Lighthouses
of
Atlantic Canada

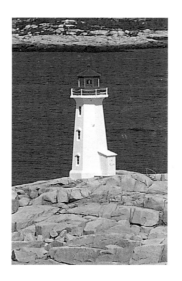

David M. Baird

RED DEER PRESS

5 4 3 2 1

THE PUBLISHERS
Red Deer Press
813 MacKimmie Library Tower
2500 University Drive N.W.
Calgary Alberta Canada T2N 1N4

CREDITS
Cover and text design by Ben Kunz, Kunz Design.
Special thanks to Laura Golins, Dan Krut, and Greg Madsen.
Printed and bound in Canada by Friesens for Red Deer Press.

PHOTO CREDITS
Cover photo (Cape Spear, Newfoundland), title page photo (Peggy's Point, Nova Scotia), and photo opposite contents page (Pictou Bar, Nova Scotia) by David M. Baird. All other text photos by the author and from the David M. Baird Collection, courtesy of the Public Archives of Canada. Other photographs and illustrations from or contributed by: W.D. Adams, *Lighthouses and Lightships*, 1871, p. 11 (left and centre) and p. 20 (left and centre); Wendy Barrett, p.221 (above right); Canadian Coast Guard (Québec), p. 33 (above right), p. 54 (below left and right); Canadian Coast Guard (Newfoundland), p. 213 (above); Chance Bros. Catalog, p.20 (below right); Charles Cullum, p. 216; Lacy M. Green, p. 70 (above and centre); James Guptil, p. 154 (below left); David Kingstone, general assistance, National Library of Canada, p. 11 (below right), p. 192 (below left); Lew Perry, p. 201 (above), p. 202 (above), p. 203; Rita Anderson, Southwest Development Association, Newfoundland, p. 227 (below left and right); Cindy Vihvelin, p. 80 (above left); Brian Tuck, p. 215 (centre and below).

ACKNOWLEDGEMENTS
Financial support provided by the Canada Council, the Department of Canadian Heritage, the Alberta Foundation for the Arts, a beneficiary of the Lottery Fund of the Government of Alberta, and the University of Calgary.

THE CANADA COUNCIL | LE CONSEIL DES ARTS
FOR THE ARTS | DU CANADA
SINCE 1957 | DEPUIS 1957

NATIONAL LIBRARY OF CANADA CATALOGUING IN PUBLICATION DATA
Baird, David M. (David McCurdy), 1920–
Lighthouses of Atlantic Canada / text and photography by David M. Baird.
ISBN 0-88995-275-2
1. Lighthouses—Atlantic Provinces. 2. Lighthouses—Atlantic Provinces—Pictorial works. I. Title.
VK1027.A8B34 2003   387.1'55'09715   C2003-910150-9

~~~~~~

Dedication

*T*o all those individuals and associations honouring a
proud maritime tradition in Atlantic Canada by preserving and maintaining lighthouses.

Apologia

Lighthouses all over the world began to change shortly after the Second World War as ships began
to use advanced navigation systems and as computer-controlled mechanisms for lights were invented.
Gone now are the days when keepers and their families tended lights and fog alarms in neat little
compounds of red-roofed houses and service buildings. Only a few dozen full lightstations remain
in Canada—about 20 in Newfoundland and another 20 in British Columbia. Even these will probably disappear in the next few years, leaving the capes, islands, and reefs of Canada's coasts guard-
ed by lonely, unmanned towers with perhaps one small service building. Such is the nature of
progress in a world of constantly changing technologies. Nevertheless, for me, lighthouses are still
beautiful and romantic beacons of the sea with stories of danger, shipwreck, bravery, and the people
who tend the lights.

My own trips to lighthouses span more than 60 years, time to have witnessed this entire evolution. Thus, in this book, some of the photographs show lightstations in their heyday and at their
best. The description in each entry notes what has changed and is presented with the knowledge
that even the contemporary scene is liable to change again in the coming years.

Author's Acknowledgements

My interest in lighthouses began in 1935 while visiting Keeper Lauder and his family at the
Partridge Island light in Saint John Harbour. Since then, I have witnessed profound changes as the
manned stations of great technical variety and appearance of yesteryear gave way to the fewer, automated, unmanned stations of today. I am proud to have met resident keepers and their families on
lightstations on the outskirts of major ports, on lonely shores, and on remote islands—and I
acknowledge their friendly help. My only regret is that so many of them have had to give up their
way of life in recent years in the face of changing times. Lightstations are much more lonely places
without them.

No book on Canadian lighthouses would be possible without the assistance of the keepers of the
lights, the Canadian Coast Guard. Their generous and cheerful help has spanned transportation,
shared expertise, anecdotes, and good company in all the Atlantic agencies of St. John's, Halifax,
Saint John, Charlottetown, and Québec City.

Officials in public archives and museums—notably the National Archives of Canada and the
Public Archives of Newfoundland—have been most helpful, as have been the staff of Historic Sites
Canada. The research of E.F. Bush, published by that department in 1975, is a vital starting point
for any scholar of lighthouses in this country.

A special word of thanks and encouragement goes to those people working to preserve our lights,
especially the Friends of the Yarmouth Light (Yarmouth, Nova Scotia) and the Southwest Coast
Development Association (Newfoundland), who did not hesitate to share their knowledge and
resources with me. I hope they will accept my grateful thanks and take pleasure in seeing "their"
lighthouses in this book.

~~~~~~

Pictou Bar, Nova Scotia.

Contents

Île Plat (Flat Island), Gulf of St. Lawrence, Québec.

A Flash of Light on a Dark Sea

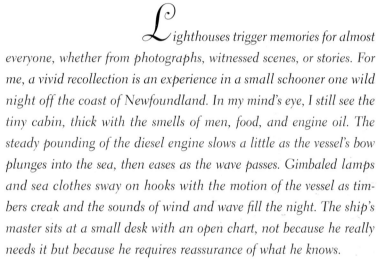

Lighthouses trigger memories for almost everyone, whether from photographs, witnessed scenes, or stories. For me, a vivid recollection is an experience in a small schooner one wild night off the coast of Newfoundland. In my mind's eye, I still see the tiny cabin, thick with the smells of men, food, and engine oil. The steady pounding of the diesel engine slows a little as the vessel's bow plunges into the sea, then eases as the wave passes. Gimbaled lamps and sea clothes sway on hooks with the motion of the vessel as timbers creak and the sounds of wind and wave fill the night. The ship's master sits at a small desk with an open chart, not because he really needs it but because he requires reassurance of what he knows.

When the time is right, he climbs the narrow steps to the wheelhouse. His mate stands on the grating with both hands on the wheel and an eye on the dimly lit binnacle, its compass card reeling back and forth as the small ship plunges and rolls. Suddenly, after hours of pushing eastward on the endless dark sea, a pinpoint of light flashes, then is gone. It flashes again three seconds later and reappears half a minute before the cycle repeats itself. At that moment, the man knows he is off Cape St. Francis. When the light comes abeam, he is confident that a southward change of course will bring him home to St. John's and safe harbour. This is what lighthouses are about.

For some people the message the lighthouse gives is "Keep off, here is danger." For others it is "Now you know where you are." And for others the message is "This way to safety and home." And for some the lighthouses hold all three messages.

No Help From Land

The pioneers who settled Canada and those who followed to establish commerce had to cross the North Atlantic Ocean, notorious for its fogs and winter storms. Even in fine weather, Canada's eastern shores were fraught with danger from hidden rocks and reefs, offshore shoals, and invisible offsetting currents. Making first landfall was especially hazardous at night and in the frequent blanketing fogs. For 200 years, until lighthouses began to mark the country's shores in the early 18th century, coastal navigation was done without assistance from land. Since then, Canadian lighthouses have been a part of a proud maritime tradition. Their story is filled with bravery and hardship, endurance and ingenuity, tragedy and happiness in a great variety of settings from remote wave-washed rocky islands to city suburbs.

Lighthouses Everywhere

Some Canadian East Coast lighthouses have become familiar sights on postcards, calendars, tourist literature, and promotions of things Canadian at trade fairs and exhibitions. Especially well known is the lighthouse on Peggy's Point (Peggy's Cove), Nova Scotia, on its rounded granite cape with a westering sun on the sea beyond. Another internationally recognized image is the white lighthouse tower at Head Harbour, New Brunswick, with its giant red St. George's cross.

The Atlantic provinces promote lighthouse routes along their coasts for visits to those lights accessible by land. In some places, boat tours to offshore islands are available for people interested in seabirds, marine life, and lighthouses. Major ferry routes—from the mainland to Prince Edward Island and to Newfoundland, across the Bay of Fundy, and on the St. Lawrence—carry thousands of passengers past active and restored lighthouse stations. Accounts of the Titanic disaster always include Newfoundland's Cape Race lightstation and its receipt of the first distress calls from the crippled vessel. Following the dreadful Swissair crash in 1999 off Nova Scotia, the media featured many photographs and televised images of victims' relatives standing on the shore beside the lighthouse at Peggy's Point. It is little wonder that thousands of people belong to lighthouse societies and associations dedicated to the preservation and restoration of lightstations.

Bravery and Romance in the Midst of Danger

Lighthouses are positioned at points of danger on the sea, so it is not surprising that almost every one of them has witnessed shipwrecks nearby, sometimes at the foot of the light tower itself. Many lighthouses have stories of incredible bravery as their keepers put out to sea in small boats or clambered down steep cliffs to attempt rescue of passengers and crews of foundering ships. Others have tales of hardship for keepers and their families as supplies failed to arrive. Frequent foul weather and continuous isolation meant that no help was available when accidents and illnesses occurred.

Yet for many of us, lighthouses are romantic places that induce dreams of being lighthouse keepers. We think of standing beside the light tower, watching the sea in its changing moods, with seabirds wheeling about, whales spouting offshore, ships and fishing boats passing nearby or on the distant horizon. We think of the satisfaction of keeping the light in spotless good order to help mariners safely on their way.

Most of us who visit lightstations, however, arrive on calm days when it is difficult to picture the same places in wild storms with huge waves pounding the shore and even attacking the light tower itself, the air filled with blown spume in the fury of the gale. We skip over what it must have been like to live at this place without seeing anyone else for months at a time, with fog and foul weather for weeks on end, with supply boats overdue, and with food running low. Yet we know that for most lighthouse keepers working on lightstations was a way of life they would exchange for no other. We also know that sons and daughters often followed in their parents' footsteps, with sometimes several generations of the same family manning the same station.

MODERN TECHNOLOGY TAKES OVER

Now, all over the world, modern technology is swallowing up traditional lighthouse stations. Gone are many of the great revolving lights atop graceful towers. Replacing them are automated searchlights powered by solar cells and controlled by computers, and mounted on skeleton steel towers. Only piles of rubble mark the spot where the old towers once stood and where families lived in isolation in order to keep the lights running. Crumbling stone foundations of keepers' houses are lost among the weeds. All along Canada's East Coast are places where nothing is left of formerly active lightstations. Ships can now travel from one dock to another thousands of kilometres away without ever needing land or stars or sun for navigation. To know where they are, even in deep fog or pitch darkness, officers have only to peer into radar screens, check satellite navigation instruments, and punch up coordinates on banks of computers that send course changes to automatic steering devices.

Yet despite advances in technology, comfort is given to many at sea when they recognize the distinctive shape and colour scheme of a light tower on a headland or detect a flash on the horizon at night and know exactly where they are. This is especially the case for fishing boats and coastwise traffic that still navigate using local lights. The great landfall lights still provide assurance to sea and air navigators that long voyages are nearing their ends. In settings of often spectacular beauty, in both calm and savage seas, the lighthouse remains a symbol of a courageous tradition of human ingenuity, invention, and self-sacrifice.

About This Book

Canada's East Coast is home to hundreds of lighthouses and other aids to marine navigation. This book features some 250 of them in five provinces, tells something of their individual stories, and provides directions on how to reach the more accessible examples. The form, construction, and unique visual markings used to identify specific lighthouses are discussed along with brief descriptions of the development of lighthouse technology. As background, the story of lighthouses is traced from their ancestors, primitive fires lit on headlands thousands of years ago, to the present automated unmanned stations.

SELECTING LIGHTHOUSES

My reasons for picking some lightstations over others range from their public accessibility, size, beauty of form, and technical importance to their location in settings where historically significant events have occurred.

Some East Coast lights have played prominent roles in Canadian history. Harrowing tales of shipwreck and tragedy caused lights to be built on Nova Scotia's St. Paul's Island, off the tip of Cape Breton Island, and on lonely Gull Island on the north coast of Newfoundland. Nova Scotia's Sambro Island lighthouse, on the approaches to Halifax Harbour, for example, has welcomed transatlantic and coastwise travellers for two and one-half centuries. It witnessed the arrival of

Sambro Island, Nova Scotia.

United Empire Loyalists in the late 1700s, and as part of the War of 1812, it was witness to HMS *Shannon* towing the defeated USS *Chesapeake* into harbour. For hundreds of thousands of soldiers leaving for each of the world wars, the Sambro lighthouse provided the last glimpse of Canada. For 150 years, Newfoundland's great landfall lights at Cape Race and the south end of Belle Isle provided the first glimpse of shore for ships and aircraft approaching North America. All these lighthouses welcomed immigrants to Canada.

Some lighthouses were chosen for their unusual locations, such as New Brunswick's wave-washed Gannet Rock at the entrance to the Bay of Fundy, and Québec's remote Bird Rocks in the Gulf of St. Lawrence. Other lighthouses were selected for inclusion because of their unusually beautiful form, such as the tall tapering round tower at Point Prim, Prince Edward Island, near Charlottetown. Others represent unusual structures needed to suit the location, such as those built on caissons in the St. Lawrence River estuary, Québec, and in Miramichi Bay, New Brunswick.

Still other lighthouses were chosen for their colourful daymarks. Unique examples exist at Head Harbour in southern New Brunswick, with its great St. George's cross; at West Point, Prince Edward Island, with its horizontal black stripes; and at Point Lepreau, New Brunswick, with its bright red and white stripes. Finally, a few lighthouses were chosen simply because they are readily accessible and very well known, such as Peggy's Point (Peggy's Cove), Nova Scotia. And some, of course, are simply the ones I love best, for who could visit lighthouses or write about them and not have favourites?

~~~~ Lighthouses in History ~~~~

The earliest sailors in primitive boats had no means of determining their location once out of sight of land. Not surprisingly, they travelled by day and hugged the coastline, using topographical features on the shore to find their way. Initially, prominent coastal landmarks acted as navigational aids. Eventually, tall masonry structures were built to be seen easily from the sea. But by night, mariners still faced dangers along rugged coastlines and submerged reefs. They soon concluded that lights beaming from towers could help them safely to shore. These became the first lighthouses.

BEACONS ACROSS THE AGES

In pre-Roman times, bonfires were lit on headlands and primitive stone towers to guide mariners along the coast. In their heyday, the Romans constructed approximately 100 light towers around the Mediterranean and European coasts. One of these, though in ruins, can still be seen at Dover, England, overlooking the modern harbour with its hydrofoils, air-cushion boats, and the entrance to the Chunnel.

By the mid-18th century, lighthouses had been built in many parts of Europe. These culminated during the 19th century in magnificent stone towers built on isolated, wave-swept rocks off the coast of Britain in such places as Eddystone, Bell Rock, and Bishop's Rock. In the 19th century, as world commerce rapidly increased and shipping routes spread over the world's oceans, lighthouses were built on most continent's coastlines. The rugged coastline of Atlantic Canada, the gateway to North America, was lit here and there by 1810 and well lit by 1910.

Fire beacon atop a rough stone tower at Dover, England, in Roman times. Its ruins still stand above the modern port.

The first masonry tower built on a wave-washed rock with interlocking blocks. This lighthouse built by Smeaton on Eddystone in 1759 set the pattern for lighthouse construction on exposed rocks the world over.

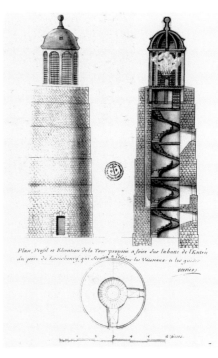

Plans approved in 1731 for the construction of a lighthouse at Louisbourg, Nova Scotia, the first lighthouse in Canada.

Seascapes—all scenic and beautiful but all hazardous to navigation.

~~~ *Canadian Lighthouse Styles* ~~~

IDENTIFYING LIGHTHOUSES

It was vital that ocean navigators be able to identify their location as they came over the horizon to their first sight of land or emerged from obscuring coastal fogbanks. Recognizable landmarks were helpful to those who knew the shoreline, but for those sailing shores unknown to them, a lighthouse was essential. When a lighthouse was sighted on an unfamiliar shore, either by day or night, it had to be specifically identified to be useful to navigation. To resolve this problem, several methods of identifying lighthouses were developed.

Initially, Canadian lighthouses were painted white so they would stand out against dark shorelines or surrounding ocean. The lighthouse platforms, lamphouses, and domed roofs were painted bright red, along with the roofs of adjacent staff houses and sheds housing engines and foghorns. These red tops set Canadian lightstations apart from most American lightstations, which had black tops.

In Canadian waters, however, the usual white towers were sometimes difficult to distinguish against snow-covered landscapes, fogbanks, or even overcast skies. On rugged coastlines in eastern Canada, where there are scores of lights, it was also necessary to identify one lighthouse from another. For day-time identification, therefore, a system of patterns on lighthouse towers, known as daymarks, was developed. These included stripes, horizontal bands, spirals, and even checkerboard squares in red or black. At night, each lighthouse flashed its light on and off in a distinctive code.

Navigators additionally used the shapes of lighthouse towers and their locations as identifiers. Tall or short; round, square, or octagonal; tapering or plain; solid or skeletal latticework; plain or ribbed with flying buttresses—these, too, were distinctive traits. Size was also important, for there is a major difference between the 30-metre (100-foot) towers at Cape Race, Newfoundland, and Cap-des-Rosiers, Québec, and the squat little lights at Cape Tormentine, New Brunswick, and Fort Amherst, Prince Edward Island. Useful, too, are their locations on particular headlands, isolated rocks or islands, bare rocks or wooded slopes, or at the ends of breakwaters or docks.

Clockwise from top left: Southwest Point, Québec; Point Prim, Prince Edward Island; Point Escuminac, New Brunswick; Mullins Point (Wallace), Nova Scotia; Pugwash, Nova Scotia.

Towers to Hold the Lights

Since the first lighthouses were erected at Louisbourg and Sambro Island, Nova Scotia, more than 200 years ago, hundreds of lighthouses have been built in Canada. They were placed on small rocky islands swept by wind and wave, in tranquil clearings on wooded points, at harbour entrances, and even in city settings. It was inevitable that a variety of materials would be used in their construction: wood, brick or stone masonry, concrete, cast iron, and even fibreglass. In some places, materials such as stone were available on site. Sometimes local forests and mills supplied timbers, sheathing, and shingles. At other sites, everything had to be shipped to a nearby safe landing and dragged up steep rocky cliffs. Several distinctive Canadian styles were developed to suit time and place.

Distinctive shapes and daymarks (clockwise from top left): Rivière à la Martre's red tower with its seaward white stripe, Cape North's cylinder with its red checkerboard, Seal Island's tapering octagon with two red bands, Cape Bonavista's square two-storey house with its red vertical stripes, Heart's Content's cylinder with its red barber-pole stripe, and Head Harbour's white tower with its red cross.

STONE TOWERS

In many places, the same rocky shores that posed dangers to shipping supplied the stone for lighthouse towers. At Rose Blanche Point, Newfoundland, for example, granite blocks were hewn in 1873 from the bedrock just below the lighthouse. Extra stone for its recent restoration came from the same source. The great limestone towers on Anticosti Island, Québec, were constructed in the 19th century from the local limestone ledges. Rubble rock near building sites was often used between brick and stone masonry walls. In some places, such as Gannet Rock, New Brunswick, towers were built of wood or other materials on massive stone foundations. Mussel shells from the beach were burned to make lime for mortar at the Cape Roseway, Nova Scotia, lighthouse in 1788. The fine-grained limestone that makes the very smooth walls of the fat cylindrical lighthouse at Red Islet, Québec, is reputed to have been brought across the Atlantic from Scotland in 1848 (left).

WOODEN TOWERS

By 1870, wood had become the most common lighthouse material because it could be supplied economically from local forests and mills. In some of the classic wooden towers, such as those at Seal Island, Nova Scotia, and East Point, Prince Edward Island (right), the heavy hand-hewn timbers are still serving well. Towers as high as 25 metres (82 feet), made entirely of wood, still mark prominent coastal features. The most common styles are tapering wooden towers from 4–25 metres (13–82 feet) high with metal and glass lamphouses on top. The smallest towers—which graced hundreds of harbours, rivers, and back channels—earned the sobriquet "peppershaker" for their square shapes, tapering sides, and squat caps.

Wooden towers can be square, hexagonal, octagonal, or even round. Other lights were housed in square wooden buildings of one or two storeys with the lamphouse protruding from the centre of the peaked roof. The lighthouses at Cape Bonavista and Cape Spear in Newfoundland are of this type, and both are preserved as historic sites. In early days, the keepers' residences were attached to the wooden towers.

BRICK TOWERS

Bricks were imported in earlier times to be used both as linings and as the main fabric of lighthouses. Some of these brick towers were later covered in coats of cement or wood sheathing to protect the masonry from the weather and salt spray. The pile of rubble marking the demolished tower at West Point on Anticosti Island, Québec, for example, is full of imported yellow firebrick. One of the most beautiful of all Canadian lighthouses, at Point Prim, Prince Edward Island (right), was originally a tapering brick cylinder that was later sheathed in wood and shingled.

CAST-IRON TOWERS

During the mid-19th century, round cast-iron towers were erected in many locations in Newfoundland and Nova Scotia. The plates were cast in Britain, brought to the nearest practical landing site, hauled up the cliffs, and bolted together. In 1856, a cast-iron tower was installed on Cape Race, Newfoundland. In 1907, it was taken apart, plate by plate, moved to Cape North on Nova Scotia's Cape Breton Island, and reassembled. In 1978, it was again dismantled and, after a complete restoration, reassembled on the grounds of the National Museum of Science and Technology in Ottawa. The Cape Pine lighthouse in Newfoundland (left), now designated an historic site, is one of the few iron lighthouses still in service.

Concrete Towers

In the early 20th century, Canadian lighthouses were commonly constructed of concrete made from locally available sand and gravel. Angular forms were easy to build, so square, hexagonal, and octagonal towers became common. Some had ribs on the corners. A series of concrete towers built with central cores and prominent flying buttresses for stability drew worldwide admiration. The old light tower at Father Point (Pointe-au-Père), Québec (left), now preserved as part of a museum complex, is an accessible example.

Caissons

Caissons (cylindrical steel shells) were sunk into sandbars where there was no rock formation in the St. Lawrence estuary, Québec, and in Miramichi Bay, New Brunswick. Deep underwater foundations were usually prepared on site, then the caisson was towed out, lowered into place, and filled with rock and concrete. Haute-Fond Prince (Prince Shoal) (below) and Île Blanche Reef (White Island), both in the St. Lawrence region of Québec, are notable examples of caisson lighthouses.

Open Steel Towers

Structural steel has been used in a variety of circumstances to build towers to support a small lighthouse on top. Slender structural steel towers, similar to radio transmission towers, now hold powerful search-light-style lamps that operate in place of, and often right beside, older wooden and concrete towers. The lighthouses at Father Point, Québec, and Cape Bonavista, Newfoundland (below), are examples.

Range Lights, Bells, and Buoys

Range lights are placed in pairs, one behind the other, so that an incoming vessel may confidently stay in the channel by keeping them in line. In other places, marking buoys bob at anchor, shifting as tides ebb and flow (below). Some have flashing lights, while others have large bells that clang out their messages as they rock back and forth in the waves. Still others carry arrays of radar reflectors. Many take their names from the dangerous shoals or reefs on which they are located.

~~~~~ *Lights and Lamps* ~~~~~

How Lighthouses Work

The development of lighthouses is a fabric woven of several threads: the towers to hold the light, the light source, the apparatus to direct the light, and the means to identify the light. The evolution from bonfires on the ground to automated high-intensity revolving lights on skeletal steel towers took 3,000 years. Each thread has a separate history, but developments in one often influenced developments in another. As you read about or visit Canadian lighthouses along the Atlantic coast, you will encounter just about every aspect of their development from the simplest little wooden tower holding a simple lamp to the most advanced lighthouse with festoons of radio antennas, radar beacons, and automatic weather-reporting devices.

The earliest source of light for beacons was a simple bonfire, sometimes built on a prominent headland, sometimes atop a rudimentary masonry tower. In the earliest formal lighthouses, batteries of candles produced the light. In the 19th century, enclosed wick lamps provided a brighter light using a variety of oils—whale, seal, fish, colzil (rapeseed), and other vegetable oils—but their flames were still not brilliant. Various glass enclosures for the lights and the lamp rooms improved the brightness.

When, in 1946, Dr. Abraham Gesner of Nova Scotia invented a way to extract kerosene oil from coal, he discovered a fuel for lamps that improved lighthouses all over the world. The next leap forward came with the invention of mantle lights, the same kind that campers use to this day. In the 1850s, electricity made an experimental appearance in a lighthouse in England, but not until the incandescent bulb became practical in the early 1900s did electric lights become common. Since then, light sources have evolved into the intense lights produced by mercury vapor, xenon, and other light-generating gases.

In Canada, the move to electricity was virtually complete by the 1950s, when the last few oil lamps were replaced. Nowadays, almost all stations run on electricity from solar cells. A few remote automatic lights still run on acetylene gas turned on and off by daylight-sensitive switches.

Reflectors and Lenses

The unaided flames used until the mid-18th century were ineffective as lighthouse beacons. To concentrate the light into beams with increased strength and range, reflectors and lenses were developed. William Hutchinson, a Liverpool harbour official, quite casually precipitated a revolution in lighthouse technology by placing a dish lined with reflecting mirrors behind the flame. This reflecting mirror system, known as catoptric, quickly developed into parabolic reflectors of polished metal that made the lights many times brighter. Reflector-equipped lights were still in use at East Point, Prince Edward Island, and Red Islet, Québec, as late as 1980, and they are preserved in place there today. Several of these lights are displayed in museums, and a wonderful multi-reflector system is maintained intact at Cape Bonavista, Newfoundland.

Tinkering with glass lenses to improve lights' brilliance began in France and England during the early 1800s, leading to a brilliant invention by Frenchman August Fresnel. In 1828, Fresnel placed a large lens in the centre of concentric rings of carefully cut and polished glass. The Fresnel lens was a great leap forward. After its invention, the company of Barbier, Bénard and Turenne of Paris quickly became the supplier of the Fresnel lens to the world. These simple lens systems became known as dioptric. In subsequent years, Thomas Stevenson added all-enclosing arrays of polished and shaped glass rings that concentrated the light radiating in all directions into a single, very powerful forward beam.

In 1845, lenses and reflectors further evolved as the company of Chance Brothers of Birmingham, England, and other inventors surrounded the central lenses with layer upon layer of reflecting and refracting prisms. The resulting lens system became known as catadioptric.

By 1900, sophisticated and vastly improved lens systems were available in a range of sizes from very small (sixth order) to 2 metres (6.5 feet) (first order) to enormous 4-metre (13-foot) -high lens systems. A hyperradial system of this type with four great lenses can still be seen in the lighthouse tower at Cape Race, Newfoundland.

The intricately sculpted and polished lens systems of the larger lights are among the most beautiful of all industrial creations. Most of them have been removed from active light towers, but a few remain in lighthouses such as the example at New Ferolle Peninsula, Newfoundland. Others, such as the old Sambro Island lens, are on display at the Nova Scotia Museum in Halifax. The Seal Island lens and lamphouse are on display beside the main road in Barrington, Nova Scotia, in a reconstruction of the top of the original tower.

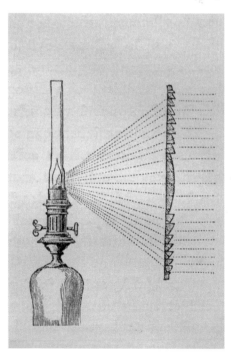

An oil-burning lamp and simple Fresnel lens. The Fresnel lens was a breakthrough in lighthouse development.

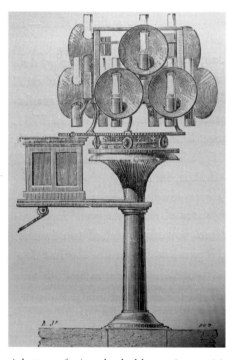

A battery of mirror-backed lamps (catoptric) of the type common in the early 19th century. An example is preserved at Cape Bonavista, Newfoundland.

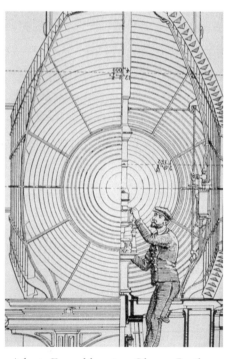

A large Fresnel lens in a Chance Brothers lamphouse, mid-19th century.

LAMPHOUSES AND WINDOWS

The housings for Canadian lamps, reflectors, lenses, and lights were brought mainly from Europe. Chance Brothers and Barbier, Bénard and Turenne were the principal suppliers. Their nameplates can still be found in many old lighthouses in eastern Canada. Their round or octagonal lamphouses with riveted copper or iron domes still adorn many principal lights. Unappealing aluminum lamphouses replaced the originals on many towers in the modernizations of the 1960s–80s. The lighthouse at Cape St. Mary's, Newfoundland, is an example.

In very simple lights, the panes of glass around the lamphouse are plain squares or rectangles of window glass. In larger lights, heavy square, rectangular, or curved plate glass panes are more characteristic. The most elegant have glass panes set in triangular or diamond frames. Though not common in Canadian lights, examples may be seen at Long Point (Twillingate), Ferryland, and Gull Island (Cape St. John), all very windy spots in Newfoundland where extra strength is needed. In addition to being stronger, helical or triangular patterns help eliminate minor blinds spots caused by the frames.

Clockwise from top left: the airport control tower-type sloping panes at Cape Spencer, New Brunswick; the flat single row of panes at St. Mary Islands, Québec; the beautiful triangular panes at Long Point (Twillingate), Newfoundland; the large curved panes at Cape Race, Newfoundland.

WINKS AND FLASHES

When beacons first became common, the lights were fixed and had a steady and continuous beam. Some had large lenses or mirrors to concentrate the beam in one direction; others were omnidirectional. They warned navigators to keep clear but gave no indication of their identity. By 1780, lighthouse engineers had set about devising characteristics by which the light itself would supply a quick and sure visual identification. They began to experiment with codes of winks and flashes specific to each light.

Flashes were produced by rotating mirrors or lenses around a central stationary lamp. With the invention of acetylene lamps and electric lights, flashes could be produced by suddenly increasing and decreasing lamp intensity. Another approach used a steady light that was punctuated with bright flashes as rotating lenses came into focus to briefly intensify the beam. Another system of interrupted or occulting lights ("winkers") was developed using a steady light that was totally eclipsed or blacked out at regular intervals by a rotating ring with one or more blinds.

Since their invention nearly two centuries ago, flashing and winking lights have been in use all over the world.

Fresnel lens from Souris, Prince Edward Island.

Round and Round

The principle of rotating lights was developed in Sweden in 1781, and by 1800 it was almost universal. Small lights were rotated by a clockwork-and-gear mechanism driven by springs that keepers wound regularly. On larger lights, turning mechanisms were run by weights that were raised by hand cranks every two to four hours. In the Cape Race lighthouse, the clockwork, with its crank and weights, remains just below the huge lenses. Lighthouse lore has it that some authorities preferred clockworks with windup times of short duration to ensure that keepers were constantly alert and on duty.

When lamps and lenses grew to be several tons of metal and glass, the simple rollers supporting them became difficult to rotate. To solve this problem, the mercury float was invented. The light system was supported on a circular cast-iron vessel that floated in a corresponding circular bath containing mercury, thus greatly reducing friction and mechanical wear. The system allowed the massive lights to turn more easily and faster to maintain a particular flashing sequence. The Cape Race light, weighing seven tons and by far the largest in Canada, still rotated on its bed of 400 kilograms (880 pounds) of mercury as late as 2001.

Beams over the Curved Sea

The curved surface of the earth restricts how far a light can be seen. For example, if you are in a rowboat, the horizon is only a few kilometres away. A bonfire on a cliff 10 metres (33 feet) high can be seen for 23 kilometres (12.5 nautical miles) out to sea. If on the same cliff you erect a light tower 20 metres (66 feet) tall—for a total height of almost 30 metres (98 feet)—visibility is extended to 42 kilometres (22.5 nautical miles). The normal visibility of Cape Race light, with its height of 52 metres (170 feet) above the sea, is 56 kilometres (30 nautical miles).

For the mariner, visibility is further extended by being above the sea on a ship's bridge or crow's nest. Indeed, from a tall ship's lookout, a very tall lighthouse may be visible from as far away as 75 kilometres (40 nautical miles). A navigator can calculate his ship's distance from a particular lighthouse by observing the moment of its appearance on the horizon and using the *List of Lights*, which includes tables of the height above the sea of each light.

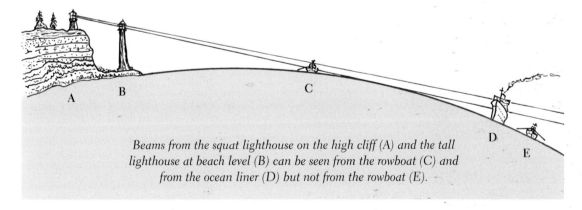

Beams from the squat lighthouse on the high cliff (A) and the tall lighthouse at beach level (B) can be seen from the rowboat (C) and from the ocean liner (D) but not from the rowboat (E).

The *List of Lights*

The Canadian Coast Guard publishes a comprehensive *List of Lights* for each of the four regions of Canada. It notes the exact location of each light, its daymark, its characteristic flashing sequence, and the frequency and code of its fog signal. The height above the sea of the source light, the height of the tower itself, and the range of the light are included. From time to time, new editions with updates are provided. Editions prior to about 1990 included dates of original construction and subsequent alterations.

Fog and Foghorns

Fog has long been the peril of the sea most feared by sailors, whether on the bridges of large ships or tossing in two-man fishing dories. Dense long-lasting fogs are common on Canada's East Coast because of temperature differences between ocean and air. Even at night, the most powerful beams produced by cleverly designed lenses and lamps cannot penetrate more than a few metres of these dense fogs.

Cannon preserved at Île Bicquette, Québec, recall a time when they were used to signal ships in fog.

Old fog horns at Bell Island, Newfoundland.

I recall once being aboard CGS *Alexander*, navigating on radar and radio in thick fog in the Atlantic off Nova Scotia. It was so dense that the bow was scarcely visible from the bridge. The first land discernible was the pier at Louisbourg showing up less than 30 metres (100 feet) away as lines started to be thrown ashore to the docking crew.

On another trip to northern Newfoundland many years ago, I was aboard the *Glencoe* as she inched her way toward Trinity in dense fog. Our whistle sounded roughly every five seconds, and I wondered why. Later I asked the captain, and he smiled and said that he was navigating through the narrow channel by listening to the echo off the nearby cliffs!

Almost as soon as lighthouses became common in the 18th century, it was realized that visual aids to navigation would have to be augmented by sounds. At first large bells were installed at lighthouses and tolled by the keepers in fog. They were not very effective, so cannons were tried with erratic results. Reed horns were developed, at first driven by hand and later by steam or compressed air. Sirens and steam whistles were installed on some stations in the mid-19th century, but it was the Canadian-invented steam diaphone that enabled controlled sounds to be consistently audible over many kilometres.

In diaphones, a slotted hollow piston moves in a similarly slotted sleeve in a rapidly reciprocating motion. A low note followed by an even lower note proved to have the best penetration in fog. Steam-driven foghorns were first used in Canada on Partridge Island, New Brunswick, in 1860, followed by the move to compressed air diaphones around 1910. Both steam and compressed air diaphones changed the lives of keepers because they required much more maintenance. Diesel-driven air compressors powered models that lasted until the 1950s and 1960s. In poor weather, lighthouse keepers and their families sometimes had to listen to the foghorn for weeks at a time. While no longer in operation, a few of the old horns are still preserved at Newfoundland lighthouses such as Bell Island and Cape Race.

Electronic foghorns replaced the old diaphone "groaners" as electrification of Canadian lighthouses followed the Second World War. At the same time, newly developed sensors flashed their radar beams across the sea and turned on the high-pitched squeals of the modern horns when fog was detected.

For lighthouse enthusiasts, one of the most interesting and beautiful natural features of summer in St. John's, Newfoundland, is watching the fog forming in the evening as cool air from the ocean steals into the harbour past the Fort Amherst lighthouse. As soon as the fog comes close, the foghorn announces its arrival.

POWER

In early times, power on lighthouse stations was supplied by the keeper himself, who carried the supplies from the landing to the tower and packed the oil up the tower to the lamps. He cranked up the heavy weights to run the clockwork that turned the light, and he even cranked the mechanical foghorn. Diesel engines came after the First World War to compress air for foghorns and generate electricity for lights and general use. By the end of the 1930s, electric motors were turning most of the rotating lights. After the Second World War, main-line electric power became widespread, reaching some island lightstations via submarine cable. For remote stations, diesel power remained the norm into the 1990s. Solar panels with banks of storage batteries became almost universal with automation occurring the 1980s and 1990s. The system generates and stores enough power to run the efficient bulbs and turn the much lighter searchlight-style beacons even in overcast weather.

Electric motor and reduction gears for old reflector light at Red Islet, Québec.

AUTOMATION

In the last 30 years, automation has transformed lighthouse operation. The micro-communities of light tower, keeper's residence, and service buildings in remote places have been replaced by the cold efficiency of computer-controlled empty stations containing only a small service building and a skeleton steel tower with an airport-type beacon. The modern low-energy, high-efficiency electric bulbs are run and even changed automatically by energy from solar panels. Electronic fog alarms are turned on and off by radar sensors and computers. Even weather conditions are sent by radio signal by remote demand. By 2000, barely more than a few dozen Canadian lightstations, all in Newfoundland and British Columbia, were still staffed.

Most Canadian lightstations, like this one at Pointe-au-Père (Father Point), are now fully automated.

This revolution in aids to navigation came through technological developments in several fields. Electrification and the development of more powerful and longer-lasting lamps made the huge Fresnel lenses unnecessary. They were replaced by much smaller molded plastic or glass lenses in searchlight housings that were light enough to be placed on skeleton steel towers. In 1953, lightweight aluminum alloy lamphouses of utilitarian design began to replace the cast-iron ones of earlier days. Some of the old tapering towers have been preserved, but they have been decapitated and now sport angular aluminum tops.

After the Second World War, marine navigators could use radar to see clearly through the densest fogs and obtain a complete picture of channels in total darkness from reflector-equipped rocks and buoys. Even the smallest pleasure boats can now be equipped with global positioning systems for a few hundred dollars. In a few seconds, captains can fix their position on the planet to within a few metres. These developments have made manned lighthouses much less essential.

Thus, the traditional lighthouse keepers, and in some cases the stations themselves, have been phased out. In their place, fewer automatic stations are sufficient. Itinerant technicians with skills unheard of in lighthouse circles a generation ago arrive by helicopter to service the lighthouses at infrequent intervals, sometimes months apart. Skeleton towers standing alone beside helicopter landing pads are the new lighthouse scene. Happily, at some lightstations, the old tower stands nearby in honorable retirement.

LIGHTHOUSE KEEPERS

Reminders of the past are still evident at the recently automated lighthouse stations of today. Old pathways, crumbling foundations of residences, and piles of rubble marking demolished towers remind visitors of a way of life that has passed.

Duties of keepers centred on keeping the light. In earlier times, oil lamps of one kind or another had to filled, wicks trimmed or replaced, glass globes polished, and lenses and reflectors kept spotless. Salt spray had to be cleaned from lamphouse windows after every storm. Weights to run the rotating lights had to be cranked by hand up the tall towers every three to four hours. Maintenance of the station, from minor repairs to the endless painting of steps, walls, and buildings was part of the duty list. Fog alarms had to be operated in bad weather. When steam-driven diaphones were introduced, furnaces had to be lit and a supply of coal made ready. Still later, diesel-driven air compressors had to be maintained and monitored continuously, perhaps for many days at a time. The weather was always with the keeper and his family as they kept a lookout to sea. In really severe Atlantic storms, the stations shook as giant waves inundated living quarters and even reached the tops of the lights.

At one time, keepers' lives were as varied as their stations. On the pillar lights of the St. Lawrence estuary and on the tiny bare-rock islands of Gull Rock, Nova Scotia, and Gannet Rock, New Brunswick, where the lightstation buildings occupied every centimetre of available space, there was nowhere for keepers to go. At remote stations, the big event was the weekly or monthly service visit by Coast Guard ship or helicopter. In contrast, at less remote stations such as Bell Island, Newfoundland, the keeper and his wife maintained a beautiful summer garden with lots of company and groceries only a few minutes away.

During the 19th century, isolation was often virtually complete, with no telephones, radio, or electricity. Keepers lived in cramped quarters in the bases of the towers themselves. When illness and accidents occurred, outside aid was only available by rowing across miles of sea in open boats. In the last half of the 20th century, life on Canadian lightstations became vastly more comfortable for keepers. Communications of several kinds came with electricity, as did refrigeration, radio, and even television. Duties also became lighter because dependable electric lights needed little attention, and electric motors drove the rotating lights. Housing was comfortable and included separate quarters for assistant keepers.

Schooling of lighthouse children was often started by the keepers' wives, using Department of Education curricula or lessons of their own devising. For higher grades, children had to study ashore for months at a time. Family tradition played a powerful role for people of the lights. Children learned to carry

A lighthouse keeper clears the sunshades at the Île Bicquette station.

out the keeper's chores and, along with their mothers, they often took over the keeper's responsibilities in emergencies. When the keeper retired, family members became logical successors. Some families thus provided lighthouse keepers for generation after generation, as in Québec at Île Verte, and in Newfoundland at Cape Spear and Cape Race.

Many hundreds of keepers have manned the lights over the more than two centuries of Canadian lighthouse history. Self-sufficiency and an ability to bear the isolation were essential, as was a dedication to the safety those in peril. Keepers needed to be able to improvise in all sorts of circumstances when equipment failed, rescues were required, or family illness arose. The best lighthouse keepers were almost all married to devoted and supportive partners.

Despite low pay, long hours, isolation, and frequent bad weather, there were always long waiting lists of people wanting to be lighthouse keepers. Now, with hundreds of them put ashore by automation, many long to be back at their old stations beside the sea with all its moods and with the satisfaction of serving those who go out to sea in ships.

Range light at Pointe Noire, Saguenay River, Québec.

Lighthouses
of
Québec

Québec has several hundred kilometres of diverse coastline, from the rugged cliffs of the Precambrian Shield along the north shore of the St. Lawrence to the low limestone flats of Anticosti Island. The province's lighthouse history is as diverse as its coastline and directly connected on the one hand to the story of settlement, the fisheries, and intercoastal trade, and on the other hand to naval history and major commerce.

The first European explorers arrived in the St. Lawrence estuary in the early 16th century, tentatively making their way upriver between islands and sandbars by day and anchoring for safety at night. Today, huge cruise ships, giant container vessels, and freighters of many nationalities confidently navigate the same waters. Québec City and Montréal have developed into major sea ports, and the St. Lawrence Seaway is the main highway of commerce into the interior of North America.

By 1770, the English and the French had largely resolved their disputes over Canada, and settlement to the west of the mouth of the St. Lawrence had begun in earnest. Ships loaded with immigrants and commerce, having survived the Atlantic crossing and the marine perils of Newfoundland and Nova Scotia, went up river past Anticosti and the Gaspé Peninsula only to encounter the islands and shifting sandbars and currents of the St. Lawrence. By 1800, numerous shipwrecks made it painfully clear that lighthouses were urgently needed. The captains of naval vessels, often on exploratory and survey missions along these coasts, also regularly reported on the desperate need for lighthouses. In 1809, the first light was erected on Île Verte (Green Island), where it remains to this day, the third oldest surviving light in Canada.

In 1830, a lighthouse was constructed at Pointe des Monts on the north shore, at a place in the river widely regarded as the point at which the real sea begins. In 1831, another light was built on Southwest Point on Anticosti Island. Next came a limestone tower at Heath Point on the eastern tip of Anticosti, in 1835, and another at Stone Pillar in mid-river, not far below Québec City, in 1843. Île Bicquette on the south shore, below Île Verte (Green Island), followed in 1844, and then Red Islet's massive stone tower off the mouth of the Saguenay in 1848.

While these few lights, scattered along several hundred kilometres of coastline, were a massive step forward, they were also reminders of how woefully inadequate the lighthouse system remained. As mapping of the lower St. Lawrence continued, it became more apparent that the navigable channels running between long sandbars and numerous islands made navigation hazardous, especially for the sailing ships of the time. The Canadian was wrecked below Québec City in 1857, and a number of serious naval losses further emphasized the need for continued action. Several famous lights appeared in 1858, notably in Newfoundland at Belle Isle South and in Québec at West Point on Anticosti Island and at Cap-des-Rosiers, site of the tallest light in Canada, on the tip of the Gaspé Peninsula. Pointe-au-Père (Father Point) was lit in 1859, and it later became the principal pilot station for ships entering and leaving the St. Lawrence River.

After 1860, new construction was slow but steady, and by the First World War, the St. Lawrence was considered a well-marked waterway. The ramming and sinking of the Empress of Ireland *in 1911, just below Pointe-au-Père (Father Point), with the loss of 1,000 lives, nevertheless served to emphasize that serious accidents could still happen.*

When the Seaway opened in 1956, the St. Lawrence River suddenly became the principal marine highway into the heart of North America. Fishing vessels and coastwise marine traffic would still play a role in the lighthouse story, but increasingly the procession of oceangoing ships—ore carriers, container vessels, bulk tankers, international tramp steamers, and cruise ships—would come to characterize the waterway as we know it today. Where sailing ships once tacked back and forth on their way upriver, anchoring at night for safety, modern marine traffic now easily traverses these waters in all weather conditions.

Ships today have the advantage of global positioning satellite systems, radar "sight," and even traffic control stations. Captains no longer depend on colourful towers and flashing lights. This change has been accompanied by universal automation of lighthouse functions so that even remote lightstations have no one there to witness the ships passing. With declining use, many stations have been abandoned. Others are now no more than skeleton steel towers with airport-type beacons powered by batteries charged by solar panels and visited once or twice a season by helicopter-borne technicians. Thankfully, in many locations, old lighthouses are being taken over by private groups who lovingly restore and maintain them. Several stations along the south shore of the St. Lawrence are now commercial establishments with fees charged to park and climb the towers.

Most eastbound travellers from Québec City take the Trans-Canada Highway, Route 20, along the south shore of the St. Lawrence River. Unfortunately, it is too far enough back from the shoreline for tourists to enjoy most of the maritime flavor of the St. Lawrence's scenery. From the old road, Route 132, much nearer to the sea, however, the south shore view is of the low shoreline with wide tidal flats commonly covered with large glacial boulders from the Canadian Shield, while the north shore view is of high rugged cliffs in the distance across the river. Lighthouses and other aids to navigation reflect the two different topographies.

St. Lawrence River
Upper North and South Shores

$\mathcal{T}$*he north shore of
the St. Lawrence River below Québec City is one of the most difficult
of all the routes in this book because the lighthouses are far apart and often located
off the highway on inaccessible points or islands. In the extreme eastern sections, the
lighthouses are in the wilderness beyond the end of the highway. These lights are
nevertheless presented because they include some notable stations, most of which
can be reached by the adventurous. The south shore of the St. Lawrence River,
on the other hand, has lighthouses, buoys, and markers on sand banks and
offshore islands. Many of them are readily accessible, and some are
even commercialized visitor centres.*

Québec City ▸

The Coast Guard depot for Québec's Laurentian region in Québec City displayed a neat red and white lighthouse in the forecourt as a symbol of purpose. It was moved from Pointe à la Renonnée (Fame Point) in 1979 and returned there in 1997. Another short tower was installed on the waterfront of the Coast Guard depot below the ramparts of Québec City, where service vessels and helicopters are based. *(See Pointe à la Renonnée (Fame Point), page 53.)*

Cap au Saumon (Cape Salmon) ▸

The Cap au Saumon lighthouse, built in 1894, is an octagonal white tower about 14 metres (46 feet) high. Its aluminum lanternhouse is octagonal and angular-looking, and painted the usual red with flat windows. In its heyday, this was a classic remote lightstation with two keepers' houses, a service building, a fog alarm, a power building, and a long boat ramp, all with connecting stairways painted red. The light is now automated and unmanned. For many years, it has been supplied by mainline hydro that follows a rudimentary road and trail from Route 136.

This lighthouse stands on a small flat shelf above the steep shoreline, backed by the high wooded hills of the Precambrian Shield that lie between it and the shore road, about 10 kilometres (6 miles) west of St. Simeon.

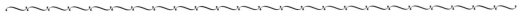

Cap de la Tête au Chien (Cape Dogs) ◄

Cape Dogs lies farther down the north shore, much farther back from the main road, Route 136. The site is in spectacular surroundings, but it is difficult to access on its patch of glaciated Canadian Shield rocks rising in steep rounded surfaces from the sea. A helicopter pad and some lower service buildings are located just above the wave-washed rocks. A walkway with 325 red steps leads up the hill to the keepers' houses and the lighthouse. Even though its white tower is only 11 metres (36 feet) high, its light stands about 60 metres (197 feet) above water level and shines its beam far out to sea. The lighthouse looks a little dumpy with its standard-sized lanternhouse on a short concrete base. The lightstation is now unmanned and completely automated.

With all those steps and many roofs, you cannot help but marvel at the amount of red paint that the keepers must have had to apply each year.

Île Blanche Reef (White Island) ▼

One of the pure pillar lights in Canada stands in 6 metres (20 feet) of water in the channel of the St. Lawrence opposite Île Verte (Green Island). It is about halfway between Rivière-du-Loup on the south shore and Tadoussac, at the mouth of the Saguenay River, on the north shore. It replaced Lightship No. 22, east of White Island.

The steel shell was designed and built at the Lauzon shipyards in 1954 and was successfully towed out, positioned, and anchored in 1955. It must have been a picturesque convoy as a Coast Guard vessel, four tugs, and the floating caisson moved down the river. They had to arrive at slack tide to avoid tidal currents and then move into exact position over the prepared foundation on the river bottom. Seacocks were opened, and the 4,000-ton caisson settled into position before being fastened to the bottom with 13-centimetre (5-inch) square stainless steel pins some 3.5 metres (12 feet) long. The whole cylinder was filled with ballast stone, and a reinforced concrete structure, four storeys high, was built on top.

The caisson is a wasp-waisted steel cylinder with the narrow part at water level to break up winter and spring ice. Its light atop the structure, some 22 metres (72 feet) above the water, is visible for more than 40 kilometres (25 miles). In later years, it cut a curious figure with a helicopter landing pad on its top with its rotating beacon peeking out below. (The lighthouse itself is not listed in the 1998 Canadian Coast Guard *List of Lights*, but its location is nevertheless still marked.)

Life on pillar lights was particularly difficult, even in fine weather, because there was nowhere to walk or run, no gardens except a window box or two, no fishing nearby, and no casual visitors. Most were lonesome lightstations too small to accommodate families. On some pillars, the views of the distant fields, forests, and even cars on the roads must have been particularly frustrating for lighthouse keepers.

ÎLE ROUGE (RED ISLET)

On a map of Canada, the St. Lawrence River appears to be a wide clear passageway into the continent. In fact, it requires very careful navigation, for it has many reefs, shoals, and small unexpected islands. Two of these hazards, Prince Shoal and Red Islet, brought many an unwary vessel to grief in the channel off the mouth of the Saguenay River. The tidal currents in this region of the St. Lawrence "are so very irregular that Vessels are frequently deceived as to their Situation" said one late 18th-century report (after Bush, p. 57).

A stout, smooth-walled stone tower was completed on Red Islet in 1848. According to lighthouse lore, its large beautifully fitted blocks were shipped from Scotland at a time when immigrant ships needed a heavy ballasting cargo. Brick was used inside the stone tower with a masonry arch supporting the light platform. The catoptric light system that backs the Red Islet light is one of the last of its kind in Canada. The old clockwork mechanism remains with the shaft for the weights going down one side. The original fourteen-sided lanternhouse has 72 panes of polished glass in three tiers inside a red metal frame under its polygonal roof. A ventilation cap on top supports an arrow-and-feathers weather vane.

This beautifully finished stone tower's 18-metre (59-foot) height is partly disguised by its stout shape and horizontal ribs. Its broad, flat, many-sided lamphouse, where the old reflector turned all those years, adds a sense of history. This is one of my favorite lighthouses in the whole of Canada.

The Red Islet lighthouse is accessible only by boat, but it is well worth the trip. Excursions now go out to it from Tadoussac in summer.

Revolving catoptric (reflector) at Red Islet, Québec.

Haut-Fond Prince (Prince Shoal) ▶

Prince Shoal is a sandy shallow area just below water level in the St. Lawrence River, off the mouth of the Saguenay River. Lighthouse builders solved problems posed by shoals in different ways. They anchored lightships, really floating lighthouses, on or near hazards. They drove pilings or steel stilts deep into the sandy bottom to support lighthouses above the water. They sank caissons into the soft bottom. *(See White Island, page 34.)*

The caisson installed on Prince Shoal in 1964 was designed to safely withstand 8-metre (26-foot) waves and carefully shaped with a "wasp waist" to break up drifting river ice in winter and spring. It was soon to be sorely tried and tested, when, on December 25, 1966, a wild storm, perhaps the worst of the century, lashed the St. Lawrence. On Prince Shoal, the three keepers watched in horror as waves mounted higher than the platform. Their isolated perch began to shake, windows caved in, and destruction spread through the upper level. When the waves reached 12 metres (39 feet), they sent out a distress signal and were rescued by helicopter half a day later, when weather permitted. By storm's end, the Prince Shoal lighthouse was a shambles with even the lamphouse broken.

A repaired and strengthened Prince Shoal lighthouse now sits atop its round caisson with all station functions carried out in a round house above the first platform. Its light tower was placed off to one side and its roof extended outward to make a slightly larger landing pad for helicopters. Its round steel tower with four red bands leads upward to a lamphouse with inward-sloping glass panes and a flat roof. Its fog alarm is unusual in that it has three horns which blow in sequence, pointing in different directions. Prince Shoal was the site of an experiment with xenon bulbs of some 32 million candlepower each, but they proved to be too brilliant and are now only used during very dull weather. Most of the time, ordinary incandescent bulbs are adequate.

Pointe Noire (Saguenay River Mouth) ◀

A square skeleton tower, typical of range lights in the area, stands at the end of the point at the mouth of the Saguenay River. Many traditional lightstations and range lights have been replaced with structures of this kind. The lightstation is located on the northeast side of the river mouth and visible from Route 138.

Pilier de Pierre (Stone Pillar)

A small rocky outcropping in the St. Lawrence, just below Île d'Orleans, is capped by a grey stone tower built in 1843 of smoothly fitted blocks with a single enlarged course near the bottom. This is surmounted by a stone platform, double-curved outwardly inclined railings, and a tall rather plain lanternhouse. It is sometimes compared to the Red Islet lighthouse, which was built about the same time but does not have the same quality.

Living conditions for lighthouse keepers must have been dreadful with no other buildings, nowhere to go, and a cold dank tower to live in. Long since automated, it is maintained for the navigation season, from April to December. Stone Pillar is accessible only by helicopter or boat.

GRANDE ISLE KAMOURASKA

The south shore of the St. Lawrence from Québec City to Rimouski is fraught with rocky islands, some standing among sandy shoals and tidal flats. Grande Isle Kamouraska is along the outer edge of these, about 35 kilometres (22 miles) upstream from Rivière-du-Loup. Automation has reduced this station to a skeleton tower and airport beacon. The old lighthouse tower, built in 1862, and the residence, added in 1913, were sadly decrepit when this photograph was taken in 1980. The hills of the Canadian Shield lie in the distance across the St. Lawrence.

Le Long Pèlerin (Long Pilgrim) ▾ and Île du Pot à L'Eau-de-Vie (Brandypot Island) ▸

Opposite Rivière-du-Loup, several long narrow islands and shoals divide the St. Lawrence River into the North and South Channels. The Brandypot lighthouse, on the farthest downstream of these islands, faces south into the South Channel. Farther upriver, Long Pilgrim and Grande Isle Kamouraska, close to the south shore, face north into the same channel.

Both Brandypot and Long Pilgrim were built in 1862 with the same pattern: a massive round brick tower about 12 metres (39 feet) high emerging from the peak of the roof of a square structure with a small extension on one side. The towers were brick cylinders, later covered in cement, which flared out at the top to support the platform. The octagonal lantern-houses were supported on iron bases, the whole protected by heavy iron railings and surmounted by riveted domes with wind vanes on top. When I visited in 1982, lighthouse functions were carried out by automatic lights on steel latticework towers. Another steel tower beside the Brandypot tower once housed an experimental wind generator.

The building at Long Pilgrim was in poor

shape then, awaiting demolition that followed a short time later. The story at Brandypot is a much happier one. In recent years, a local society has restored the old lighthouse, and it stands as a rather beautiful monument to what volunteers can do to save Canada's heritage. Tours to it and its surrounding bird sanctuary are offered in summer from Rivière-du-Loup. A limited number of visitors can be accommodated over night in the old lighthouse itself.

Île Verte (Green Island) ▶

The third oldest lighthouse in Canada still in its original form stands on a low rocky point on the seaward side of Île Verte. It is located opposite the village of L'Isle-Verte, just off the Trans-Canada Highway, 29 kilometres (18 miles) north-northeast of Rivière-du-Loup. Service began in 1809, and for more than 20 years, this was the only light on the St. Lawrence.

Construction on the original circular stone tower, with its twelve-sided lanternhouse and battery of 13 lamps, was started 1806 but not completed until 1809. When its first keeper died in 1827, a young apprentice pilot and seaman of Scottish descent, Robert Lindsay from Québec City, was appointed to replace him. Thus began an unrivaled family record of service that lasted until 1964, 137 years later. Generation after generation of Lindsays saw this lighthouse through weather fair and foul, and through all the evolution of lamps from primitive oil to electric. In their time, the lighthouse guided ships from brigs, barques, and schooners to modern-day luxury passenger ships, cruise ships, and enormous bulk carriers.

The venerable old lighthouse was declared a National Historic Site in 1974. It is accessible by an intermittent ferry from opposite the village of L'Isle-Verte on Route 132 and is also part of a package tour of the island.

Île Bicquette ▶

For generations, ships entering and leaving the St. Lawrence picked up and dropped off their river pilots at Father Point (Pointe-au-Père). Twenty-two kilometres (12 nautical miles) upriver to the southwest, they avoided a group of islands some 5.5 kilometres (3.5 miles) offshore, the outermost of which contained the Île Bicquette lightstation. A beacon for many miles in each direction, its massive round masonry tower is about 23 metres (76 feet) high with a wood cladding. Its round red platform supports a classic Barbier, Bénard and Turenne round lamphouse with curved glass windows, a large ventilation cap, and a weather vane. Its thick masonry walls are evident in its deep-set windows at each level.

In 1980, cannons were still on the grounds, left from the days when they fired fog warnings. Parts of the old gas mantle lamps were inside the lighthouse. The original first-order Fresnel lens still rotated in its cage atop the tower as it had for nearly a century and a half. An unusual feature was the red light showing in one sector to warn of shoals in that direction. A tall radio mast and electronic foghorns foretold of the coming automation, which was completed by 1981. Some of the buildings were dismantled soon thereafter and removed.

This beautiful old lighthouse, built in 1843–44, was one of three erected below Québec City in response to petitions by ship owners and mariners. It is accessible only by water.

Pointe-au-Père (Father Point)

It was November 1940 as MV *Kaipaki* cautiously felt her way through a driving blizzard toward shore to pick up the St. Lawrence river pilot at Father Point. She had just run the gauntlet of submarines and raiders in the eastern Atlantic and the Gulf of St. Lawrence. A deckboy had been ordered down from the crow's nest and sent to the bow to help a seaman peer through the slanting snow and the grey seas for the pilot boat. The windblown boom of the lighthouse foghorn sounded out of the murk as the two huddled against the railing, trying to keep warm. Eventually, the pilot boat loomed from the obscurity, and the river pilot clambered aboard. I was that deckboy, and that was my introduction to the famous Father Point lightstation. It was another 40 years before I actually saw the lighthouse itself.

The first lighthouse was constructed in 1859, destroyed by fire in 1867, and immediately replaced by another wooden tower that lasted until 1909. That year, one of Colonel W.D. Anderson's famous concrete towers, complete with flying buttresses, came into service. Its second-order Fresnel lens sent its beams 25 kilometres (16 miles) out over the St. Lawrence. In 1980, its functions were taken over by a steel lattice tower and airport beacon, and the old tower was left to deteriorate.

Now the old tower is blind and mute, its lens covered against the sun and its lighthouse duties usurped by the adjacent skeleton tower. It was designated a national historic site in 1974. Happily, the station is being restored and operated by the cooperative association Le Musée de la Mer de Pointe-au-Père. The grounds are decorated with old anchors, cannons and other relics, picnic tables, and even a children's playground. The keeper's house has been converted into a museum. For a fee you can climb the restored tower to the light platform.

This historic station, for so many years the pilot station where freighters and liners picked up and dropped their St. Lawrence river pilots, is readily accessible by a short side road from the main coastal road, Route 132, just east of Rimouski.

St. Lawrence River Lower North Shore, Gulf of St. Lawrence, and Gaspé Peninsula

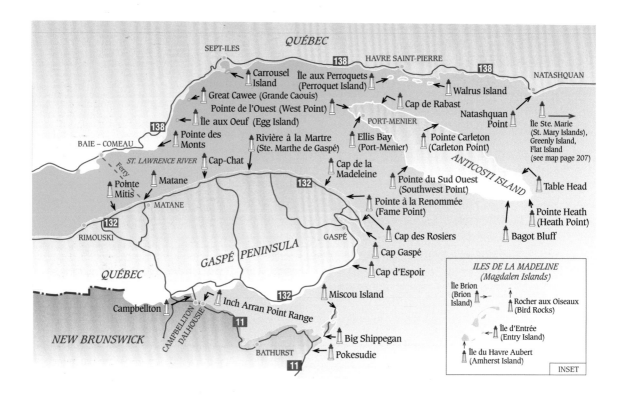

*T*he St. Lawrence
River estuary widens below Tadoussac and Rimouski to
eventually become the Gulf of St. Lawrence. Lighthouses are scattered along the
Canadian Shield, which forms the north shore all the way to the Strait of Belle Isle and the
coast of Labrador. Some of these lighthouses are accessible from the coastal highway,
Route 138, that extends as far as Natashquan. Some are on islands offshore.
Beyond the end of the highway, access is only by air or sea. Lighthouses
are also located at regular intervals along the south shore east
from Rimouski and the famous river pilot station at
nearby Father Point. They are all accessible from
the main shore road, Route 132,
around the Gaspé Peninsula
to Bay Chaleur.

POINTE DES MONTS

The Pointe des Monts lightstation is on the north shore of the St. Lawrence River estuary, about 20 kilometres (12 miles) east of Godbout on Route 138. For 81 years, the Fafard family, fathers and sons in succession, tended the lighthouse. Still largely in its original form, the massive round tower measures about 27 metres (89 feet) high and some 12 metres (39 feet) in diameter at the base. It tapers to 6 metres (20 feet) at the platform with walls almost 2 metres (7 feet) thick at the bottom and 60 centimetres (24 inches) thick at the lantern level. Until a separate residence was built in 1912, keepers lived in the tower.

When construction began in 1829, the contractors tried using local granite, but it proved difficult to work. Thereafter, they ferried limestone downriver from near Montréal. The polygonal copper lantern was over 3 metres (10 feet) in diameter and 2 metres (7 feet) high to accommodate an array of 13 Argand lamps, each with its own polished reflector, which burned sperm oil. A new lamp and a Fresnel lens system were installed at the end of the century.

The old white tower is nicely set off by its daymark of two broad red horizontal stripes and the keeper's residence with its bright red roof. Unusually large scrolled supports for the roof are still apparent. When the tower was clad in wood and shingled, the tall windows, each with 14 panes, were framed on the outside, giving a pleasing effect. In its present setting, it is easy to forget that it was built in response to the procession of horrifying shipwrecks that dotted this unmarked coast so long ago. The lighthouse is now a museum and park.

For much of its time, Point des Monts was a remote station accessible only by sea. Now it can be reached from Route 138 by a connecting road that takes you about 11 kilometres (7 miles) to the old lighthouse. From the south shore at Matane, you can reach Godbout by ferry, and then continue on to the lighthouse.

ÎLE AUX OEUF (EGG ISLAND) ▲ AND GRANDE CAOUIS (GREAT CAWEE) ▼

Two white octagonal concrete towers stand forlorn in these views taken in 1982. These lighthouses, on Île aux Oeuf (Egg Island) and Grande Caouis (Great Cawee), are located about 25 kilometres (16 miles) apart and some 80 kilometres (50 miles) southwest of Sept-Îles (Seven Islands). Long since automated, unmanned, and stripped of service buildings, both towers still showed flashing lights all year round in 1998. Not visible from the southern (Gaspé) shore, they are located nearly opposite the Rivière à la Martre lighthouse and are accessible only by water or air.

CARROUSEL ISLAND

The early days of the Second World War brought a rude awakening to the sleepy little fishing and lumbering village of Sept-Îles (Seven Islands) on the north shore of the St. Lawrence estuary when a large airport was built for patrol of the gulf St. Lawrence and for training pilots. At the end of the war, interest in the iron discoveries, deep in the hinterlands to the north, brought a flood of prospectors, geologists (including the young author of this book), construction workers, and, in the early 1950s, railway workers. Suddenly, in 1954, after several years of feverish construction, Sept-Îles became a major shipping port. Its lighthouse, built in 1870 to aid local marine traffic along the north shore, became important as the new Labrador railway brought thousands of tons of iron ore every day for shipment to Great Lakes ports and overseas. Completion of the St. Lawrence Seaway was hastened to accommodate this new industry.

Carrousel Island is on the outside edge of the archipelago that gives the name to the bay and the city. When this photograph was taken in the early 1980s, the station was still manned, but the octagonal concrete tower with its angular 1960s aluminum lamphouse and airport beacon had already been retired. The station's functions had been taken over by the skeleton tower and the small control buildings with their computers and bank of electronic horns. The station has long since been unmanned, and parts of it demolished.

The Carrousel Island lighthouse is accessible only by water or air.

Île aux Perroquets (Perroquet Island) ▲

Mingan Islands National Park is based on a series of unusual islands that lie along the north shore of the St. Lawrence directly north of the west end of Anticosti Island. The Mingan Island archipelago is a string of erosional remnants of nearly flat limestone that laps onto the ancient rocks of the Precambrian Shield all along the St. Lawrence River valley. Here they rise a metre (3.3 feet) or so above sea level with oddly shaped stacks, hoodoos, and cliffs that are home to unusual botanical species and flocks of seabirds.

On Perroquet Island, at the west end of the national park, a white octagonal tower with a red lanternhouse on top advises ships of the treacherous shoals and islands in the vicinity. Now automated, only remnants of the lightstation remind you of the families who lived on this small island for nearly 100 years after its construction in 1888. This was an isolated station that required keepers and their families to endure months of hardship. However, they were able to look forward to the closing of the station each year over the most severe winter months, when no navigation occurred on the frozen St. Lawrence.

Access is from Havre-St.-Pierre along the North Shore Road, Route 138, and subject to national park regulations.

Walrus Island ▶

In 1919, a lighthouse was placed on a limestone island in the Mingan group opposite Havre-St.-Pierre, about halfway along the east–west length of Mingan Islands National Park. In its heyday, it was a full lightstation with a white octagonal tower and matching lanternhouse totaling some 12 metres (40 feet) high. Now operational only during the summer navigation season, this lighthouse is fully automated with its functions performed by a searchlight beacon from a steel skeleton tower about 25 metres (82 feet) high.

Access is by water from Havre-St.-Pierre and subject to national park regulations.

Natashquan Point ▶

The north shore of the Gulf of St. Lawrence is marked by major rivers draining the heavily glaciated Canadian Shield just to the north. These rivers deposit sand and fine gravel at their mouths along the sea. The Natashquan Point lighthouse is surrounded by long, sandy beaches, often black with magnetite and with incredible patterns of curving sand ridges marking former river channels and beaches.

This lighthouse was built in 1914 on a terrace just back of the shoreline bank. It is a sturdy white hexagonal tower with joined buttresses measuring 9 metres (30 feet) high. When lighthouses all along that coast and on Anticosti Island were automated, Natashquan became the monitoring station for their automatic signals. Banks of glowing lights informed the keeper of the condition of the operating parts of the remote stations and the few remaining buildings. The 1998 Canadian Coast Guard *List of Lights* lists only a year-round light here on a square skeleton tower about 8 metres (26 feet) high.

The coastal highway along the north shore, Route 138, reaches Natashquan village. The lighthouse station is on the point to the east at the southeast side of the mouth of the Natashquan River.

Île Ste. Marie (St. Mary Islands) ◀

Round, glacially smoothed granite rocks of the Canadian Shield form low islands all along the Québec north shore east from Natashquan. One such group, the St. Mary Islands, about halfway between Havre-St.-Pierre and Blanc-Sablon, on the Québec–Labrador border, was given this sturdy squat concrete tower, with its revolving Fresnel lens, in 1913. Still well preserved in 1980, the St. Mary Islands lightstation was on its way to full automation with a square skeleton tower and grey control buildings already installed and performing all the duties. It is now a seasonal light, operated from April to December when the north channel is open.

This is a lovely little tower only about 5 metres (16 feet) tall from its base to its wide concrete platform. On top, its twelve-sided lanternhouse has a single row of tall glass panes, a conical red roof, and a wind-controlled vent. Such a large lanternhouse must have contained an array of oil lamps in its original days. In the photograph, the keeper's wife, whose family came over from Newfoundland a century before to settle along this coast, stands at the door. The lightstation is accessible only by water or air. Harrington Harbour is the nearest settlement.

Île Plat (Flat Island)

This aerial view is one that mariners never saw of this outpost of navigation on the low rocky Flat Island on the north side of the St. Lawrence east of Sept-Îles. Aptly named, this small barren island has been marked with a lighthouse since 1913, but now, following automation, little remains other than a skeleton tower and airport beacon some 25 metres (82 feet) above the sea. Flat Island is accessible only by water or air.

GREENLY ISLAND

For 50 years after the first light was installed in 1878, life was routine for lighthouse keepers and their families on Greenly Island. Then, in April 1928, the eyes of the world suddenly turned to this remote island in the Strait of Belle Isle on the Québec–Labrador border. That night, during a fierce snowstorm, a large airplane crash-landed in the snowy darkness beside the light.

Two days earlier, three aviators in the German aircraft *Bremen* had set out from Ireland to attempt the first westward trans-Atlantic air crossing. Two days after takeoff, they were presumed lost. Fading hopes were giving way to despair. Hours late, running out of fuel and lost in the dark, the aviators spotted a light and decided to put down there. They landed almost completely blind beside the Greenly Island lighthouse, climbed stiffly from their damaged plane, and surprised an astonished lighthouse keeper and his family. Excitement in the outside world began when the routine weather report from the keeper had appended to it the laconic message, "German plane here."

A light had first been installed on Greenly Island in 1878. A 20-metre (66-foot) tapering wooden pyramid, with a round red lamphouse and cupola, rose from one end of the principal service building and residence. The dozen or so windows in the tower itself made it unusal. The whole station was rebuilt in 1980 as a freestanding, square steel skeleton tower some 22 metres (72 feet) high with red lattice work and a searchlight on top. It is completely automated now and operates only seasonally.

Access to this lighthouse is only by sea or air. The ferry from St. Barbe, on the west coast of Newfoundland, docks at Blanc-Sablon, just inside the Québec border, about 6.5 kilometres (4 miles) northeast of Greenly Island.

The original lighthouse constructed in 1878.

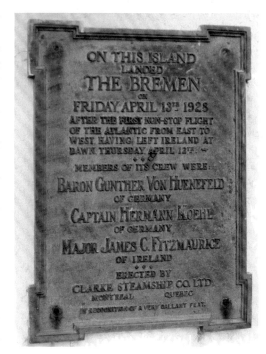

The plaque commemorating the crash-landing of the Bremen *after the first east–west trans-Atlantic flight.*

Pointe Mitis ▲

About 18 kilometres (11 miles) northeast of Mont-Joli, a reinforced concrete lighthouse stands on a sandbar called Pointe Mitis. The first light was installed here in 1874. The present automated hexagonal tower with its red top stands some 17 metres (56 feet) high. It is the major guide for coastal and river shipping halfway between Father Point and Matane, a distance of some 75 kilometres (47 miles).

The Pointe Mitis lighthouse is visible and accessible from Route 132. (Note that the national topographic maps denote the nearby village as Pointe-Métis.)

Matane ◄

The main coastal road, Route 132, passes through the centre of Matane, right beside the decommissioned lighthouse, which is now part of the local tourist information office. The lamphouse and cap appear to have been taken from an earlier light. In the archival photograph (below) is the old wooden lighthouse that stood on this spot for a century next to its new, partially finished replacement.

Cap-Chat

A lighthouse station was installed at Cap-Chat in 1871 as part of a string of lights along the south side of the St. Lawrence estuary. It takes its name from the catlike profile of a large rocky point detached from the nearby cliffs behind the old stone magazine, which was built away from the light to house the explosives for the fog guns of earlier times.

The present tower was built in 1909, and its typical Barbier, Bénard and Turenne lamphouse and third-order lens still function atop its short square wooden tower. Its position atop a high cliff allows a tower only 10 metres (33 feet) high to display its light some 40 metres (131 feet) above the sea. It is still a working light, though now automated, with a bank of electronic foghorns. Like all the lighthouses along the coastal road, the Cap-Chat station is on mainline hydro.

This station, now under the management of the Germain–Lemieux Museum, is largely intact with its several outbuildings. A large information centre has been built, and the keeper's house is a tearoom. An outdoor pioneer oven has been built, and the grounds have been beautified with gardens and tree plantings.

The Cap-Chat lighthouse is readily accessible from the main coastal road, Route 132, a few kilometres west of St. Anne-des-Monts by a short side road.

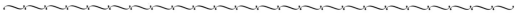

RIVIÈRE À LA MARTRE (OR STE. MARTHE DE GASPÉ)

The imposing Rivière à la Martre lighthouse, with its all-red light tower and lamphouse, sits on the edge of the coastal cliffs about halfway between Rimouski and Gaspé, on the south side of the St. Lawrence. Its rotating Fresnel lens, with its four dioptric lenses in the axis of rotation of the main glass structure, is designed to give four flashes and one gap each minute. These are clearly visible from the ground below the tower. On the seaward side, a broad white stripe from top to bottom makes a distinctive daymark. All the other buildings on the station have been painted the same red and now house various museum functions. The lighthouse station is entirely automated and is served from the local power grid. The museum admission fee allows you to climb the tower to the light.

Part of the price we pay for having local societies take over our lighthouses and save them from destruction is their inevitable commercialization. Virtually all the lighthouses along the Gaspé coast have gone through this change. While this may be regretful in some ways, rejoice that the lights are being preserved and, in most cases, well maintained.

The Rivière à la Martre lighthouse is close to the main coastal road, Route 132, and offers a splendid view of the St. Lawrence to the north.

Cap de la Madeleine ▲

Now the centre of a thoroughly commercialized operation with eager guides rushing out to meet incoming cars, the Cap de la Madeleine lighthouse stands with its round tower and highly decorated top in the midst of parking lots and museum buildings. The ambience is a far cry from the lonely lights with their devoted keepers, upon whom mariners depended on the stormy seas of the St. Lawrence estuary.

The first lighthouse was constructed on the site in 1871 and replaced with the present tower in 1906–08. It is within sight of the main coastal road, Route 132, near Rivière-la-Madeleine.

Pointe à la Renommée (Fame Point) ▶

Another solid red lighthouse on the Gaspé coast is located at Fame Point. It stands alone, a little forlorn perhaps, on a flat area above the sea with most of its original buildings now gone. A commercial operation has been built around it with replacement of original buildings as part of development. Its round iron tower supports a typical round red lamphouse with its beautiful Fresnel lens clearly visible at eye level from the parking lot. This lighthouse is billed as the most travelled lighthouse in Canada. In 1979, it was removed to Québec City, where it graced the grounds of the Canadian Coast Guard compound until 1997, when it was returned to Fame Point.

The Fame Point lighthouse is accessible from the coastal highway, Route 132, along a side road a few kilometres long, near L'Anse-à-Valleau, west of Riviére-au-Renard at the eastern end of the Gaspé Peninsula.

CAP DES ROSIERS ▶

A splendid tower some 34 metres (112 feet) tall from its base to the ball on top of the lantern-house stands on the rocky point of Cap-des-Rosiers, near the easternmost end of the Gaspé Peninsula. For more than 125 years, it was a principal light guiding ships from the Gulf of St. Lawrence into the St. Lawrence estuary. Designated a national historic site in 1974, it is the tallest lighthouse in Canada.

Its first-order catadioptric Fresnel lens, supplied in 1858 by Barbier, Bénard and Turenne, remains. The lighthouse was built for oil lamps and later graduated through a succession of improvements, including Argand lamps, gas-mantle lamps, and finally electric bulbs. Its walls are 2.3 metres (7.5 feet) thick at the base, tapering to 1 metre (3.3 feet) thick at the top. The compound masonry tower is stone (probably limestone), coated with the "finest English firebrick," as designated in the original plans, and plastered on the inside. At base level, it is about 8 metres (26 feet) in diameter, tapering to about 6 metres (20 feet) at the platform.

Windows decorate the thick walls on each of the tower's eight storeys. The tower's heavy base is set on bedrock some 2.5 metres (8 feet) below ground level. What a major undertaking construction of a light tower of this size must have been!

The Cap des Rosiers lighthouse is directly accessible from a section of the outer coastal road, Route 132 (not the bypass, Route 197) between Rivière-au-Renard and St.-Marjorique.

CAP GASPÉ ▲

A white octagonal tower with a red top is set in impressive surroundings in Forillon National Park, close to the tip of the Gaspé Peninsula. About 9 metres (30 feet) tall, the tower was built in 1873 to serve coastal shipping and local fishermen. The original lighthouse has been replaced and automated, as with all the others in the region.

This lighthouse is accessible inside the park from the coastal road, Route 132, which travels the length of the long spine of Cap Gaspé. The lightstation is located in one of the most spectacular settings in all of Canada and supplies a tremendous view from its position nearly 110 metres (360 feet) above the sea.

Cap d'Espoir

Between the town of Gaspé and the city of Chandler on the Gaspé Peninsula, the coast is fronted with rugged cliffs, part of which are the well-known outliers, Percé and Bonaventure islands. The lighthouse on Cap d'Espoir, a major beacon along that coast, is visible from several points along the coastal highway, Route 132, near the village of Cap-d'Espoir. Access is via a side road; use the power line as a guide.

The present lighthouse, built in 1939, stands near the edge of the local reddish cliffs. The houses are occupied, presumably by tenants, and the station is automated and fenced. This lighthouse is unusual in the way the three beams of its revolving light are simultaneously visible on the lanternhouse glass from time to time during each revolution.

ELLIS BAY (PORT-MENIER)

Anticosti Island, some 215 kilometres (134 miles) long and 50 kilometres (31 miles) wide, raises its limestone cliffs, wooded hills, and offshore shoals like a giant cork at the mouth of the St. Lawrence estuary. With main shipping routes passing on both the north and south sides of the island, it has long been a place of shipwreck and tragedy. As early as 1827, Royal Navy Commander H.W. Bayfield, in his surveys of the Gulf of St. Lawrence, realized that Anticosti should be marked at both ends, along with the tip of Gaspé to the south and Pointe des Monts on the north shore.

After several years of debate, principally over who should pay for these lights, a major lightstation was established in 1831 at Southwest Point, about halfway along Anticosti's south coast. In 1835, a second light was built at Heath Point on the east end of the island, and in 1858, a third was constructed on the west end. Others were added from time to time: Bagot Bluff in 1871 and, on the north side, Table Head, Carleton Point, and Cap de Rabast in 1919.

Modern range lights now lead vessels in and out of Ellis Bay and the Port-Menier harbour at the west end of Anticosti Island. The back range light used to be this small caricature of a light tower complete with solar panel.

Port-Menier at the western end of Ellis Bay is served by sea and air. Schedules vary from year to year, services are limited and some restrictions apply because the area is an ecological reserve.

Pointe de l'Ouest (West Point) ▲

The closest lighthouse station to Port-Menier, Anticosti Island's principal village, used to be at West Point, on the westernmost point of the island. A magnificent tower 33 metres (108 feet) high and tapering slightly from its 12-metre (39-foot) base was erected in 1858 on West Point's English Head. Built of local limestone and faced with imported firebrick, it bore a round lanternhouse with a railed deck and a rotating Fresnel lens system of the second order. (A similar tower can be seen at Amour Point on the Labrador coast of the Strait of Belle Isle near the Québec border.)

In 1967, after more than a century of service, the grand tower at West Point was replaced with a skeleton steel tower and airport-style beacon, and the station was demolished. By the 1970s, all that remained of a once superb lighthouse was a heap of limestone and firebrick rubble on the shoreline side of the steel tower. It is accessible by local road from Port-Menier.

Cap de Rabast ▶

In 1919, a lighthouse station was built on Cap de Rabast, on the north side of Anticosti Island. In its heyday, it was a classic lighthouse scene with its white octagonal tower, keepers' houses, and service buildings on the point. This lighthouse was one of three built on the north side of Anticosti to mark the south side of the north channel into the St. Lawrence. The light was automated in the 1970s, and when this photograph was taken in the early 1980s, the windows had been boarded up and the two single-storey buildings in front of the tower had taken over all vital functions. The low shallow shores with their extensive reefs protect the point from storm waves, which break well out.

The Cap de Rabast lighthouse is accessible on the woods roads from Port-Menier.

POINTE CARLETON (CARLETON POINT) ▲

One of the three lighthouses built in 1919 is at Carleton Point, about halfway along the north shore of Anticosti Island. Its 12-metre (39-foot) tower stands on limestone cliffs along the heavily wooded north slopes of the island. The station was automated in the 1970s.

The Carleton Point lighthouse is accessible from the network of woods roads on Anticosti.

TABLE HEAD ▲

A somewhat similar tower, also built in 1919, stands on the cliffs at Table Head, well along the shore of Anticosti Island toward its eastern end. The limestone cliffs along these shores are incredibly rich in fossils. Visitors come from all over the world to collect and study them (under permit). Access is from the woods roads that run east–west most of the length of Anticosti.

Pointe Heath (Heath Point) ▲

Only a heap of rubble remains of the 25-metre (82-foot) tower that was erected in 1835 on Heath Point at the east end of Anticosti Island. Built of local limestone and imported brick, its light shone east over the gulf, diverting traffic north or south around Anticosti. During its long history, the lightstation had the usual succession of oil lamps leading to a rotating second-order lens system. A skeleton tower about 30 metres (98 feet) away from the ruins of the old tower, with an airport beacon, has replaced the original tower. In 1980, small prefab buildings housed generating units with automatic controls, while the adjacent keepers' houses and service buildings were rapidly disintegrating. Complete automation with solar panels and batteries followed.

The Heath Point light is accessible only with some difficulty from the end of the Anticosti road system or by sea.

Bagot Bluff ▶

A square skeleton tower 15 metres (49 feet) high stands on the northwest side of South Point on Anticosti Island. It marks the site of the old Bagot Bluff lightstation, first lit in 1871. In later years, a large double keeper's house with lots of gingerbread stood beside a white tower with flying buttresses. By 1980, the house was derelict, the tower decapitated, and the station deserted. Now little is left but an automated airport beacon. Together with lights at Fame Point and Cap des Rosiers on the south side, Bagot Bluff marks the margins of the south channel into the St. Lawrence. Inquires should be made in Port-Menier about access on the woods roads on Anticosti Island.

Pointe du Sud Ouest (Southwest Point)

In 1831, Southwest Point became the site of the first lighthouse built on Anticosti island. Situated near shipping lanes on the south side of the island, it was constructed from the abundant nearby limestone and sand. Its massive 25-metre (82-foot) tower supported the first rotating light on the St. Lawrence. Initially, it burned sperm oil but soon changed to more economical and efficient fuels. Southwest Point's light, about 30 metres (98 feet) above the sea, was visible for 25 kilometres (16 miles).

By the 1970s, the station had been virtually abandoned, and the gutted tower, still magnificent in its old age, stood gaunt and empty. Close to the shore, a small lonely graveyard among the weeds reminds visitors of the time when many sailors perished offshore and keeper's families died of untreated diseases. Archival records show that for several years a priest made an annual spring visit to bury the dead that washed ashore during the previous winter.

For a time, a skeleton tower with an airport beacon took over lighthouse functions. By the 1990s, the Southwest Point lightstation was abandoned altogether. The site is accessible on the network of woods roads on Anticosti Island.

Île du Havre Aubert (Amherst Island) ▸
The Magdalen Islands, standing well out in the
Gulf of St. Lawrence, witnessed scores of shipwrecks during the first half of the 19th century.
In addition to their challenging position in the
main shipping lanes, the long low sandbars
joining the islands were impossible to see in
the welter of breaking waves and blown spume
during storms. Five lighthouses had been built
by 1875, and, from time to time since then,
other aids to navigation have been added. The
present-day Magdalen Islands are the centre of
a substantial fishing industry. Salt is also
mined deep beneath one of these islands.

The islands are served by car ferry from Souris, Prince Edward Island, and by airlines from the
mainland.

A light was placed on the south point of Amherst Island in 1871. In this 1960s photograph, its successor displays a white hexagonal tower and rotating Fresnel lens system above the typical red cliffs,
which are similar to the rocks of Prince Edward Island. Bathers enjoy the shallow warm water below
the old lighthouse, long since modernized and automated. Access is by local road.

Île d'Entrée (Entry Island) ▸
Entry Island, on one side of the main Magdalen island
group, had its own lighthouse by 1874. Its successor, an
octagonal concrete tower, now automated, continues to
send out its beacon light from the stark lamphouse
installed in the 1960s.

Entry Island was settled mainly by English-speaking
families, and the language persists with their descendants.
Access is only by air or sea.

Maintaining the Entry Island light.

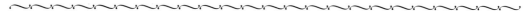

Île Brion (Brion Island)

Brion Island lies about 15 kilometres (9 miles) north of the main Magdalen Island group. Its light-house was a latecomer in the Magdalens array, arriving in 1905. By 1980, the lighthouse, standing alone with its flashing electric light, had become a favorite refuge for young travellers wanting to get away from it all. Otherwise, technicians arriving by helicopter to service the automated light were the lighthouse's only visitors. Access is by air and sea.

Rocher aux Oiseau (Bird Rocks)

A group of small islands, ledges, and shoals lies about 25 kilometres (16 miles) northeast of the main group of the Magdalens. These are directly astride the main route from the Atlantic Ocean through the Cabot Strait and into the St. Lawrence River system. The largest of these small islands is Great Bird Rock, an erosional remnant with receding cliffs of soft red sandstone and conglomerate averaging 30 metres (98 feet) high and rising steeply from the shoreline. Scattered along the cliffs are ledges, nooks, and crannies that in summer make ideal nesting sites for many thousands of gannets and other seabirds.

In his monumental survey of the Gulf of St. Lawrence in the 1830s, Captain W.D. Bayfield of the British Admiralty described the Bird Rocks as a very difficult place. After a tough climb to the top, lighthouse builders chose the least exposed indentation and built a small pier and ramp up the adjacent gully. Even with this, the Bird Rock light could be serviced only in the calmest weather, usually during short periods in July and August. By 1870, the station was complete with a 15-metre (49-foot) wooden tower equipped with a second-order, Barbier-made, Fresnel lens and oil lamp.

Since then, the typical evolution through various types of oil lamps ended with the electrification of the light in the 1960s. The original wooden structure was replaced with a hexagonal tower with a solid concrete bottom and a shingled top supporting a red octagonal lamphouse of the plain modern design. In the early 1980s, the lighthouse was still kept by two keepers who alternated on two-week shifts with another crew. Now the lightstation is unmanned and accessible only by helicopter.

Musquash Head, New Brunswick.

Lighthouses
of
New Brunswick

New Brunswick has two entirely different coastlines. The southern shore is steep and rocky with deep cold water constantly surging and mixing in the extremely high tides. The east coast along the Gulf of St. Lawrence is shallow and sandy with warm waters, long off-shore sandbars, and miles of beaches. Each has a distinctive maritime history.

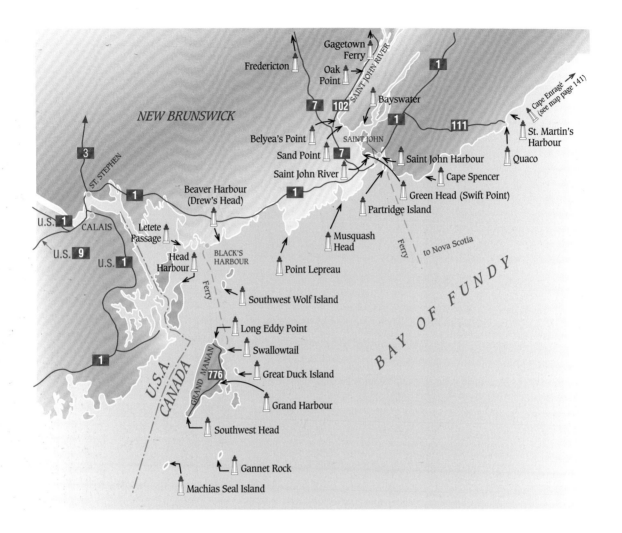

The southern New Brunswick shore
along the Bay of Fundy forms one side of the main shipping route into Saint John, one of
Canada's principal seaports. When United Empire Loyalists flooded the region in the late 1700s, navigation
aids were desperately needed to guide the small sailing vessels through deadly tidal currents and dense
fogs. With few alternate harbours or inlets to provide refuge, marine disasters were common. Not
surprisingly, major lighthouses were soon constructed. The first was constructed in 1791 on
Partridge Island at the entrance to Saint John. It was followed by Brier Island in
1809 and Seal Island in 1830 in Nova Scotia, and Gannet Rock in 1831
and Swallowtail, Grand Manan, in 1860 in New Brunswick. Since
then, hundreds of local lighthouses, channel markers, and
buoys have been installed.

GANNET ROCK

A beautiful old lighthouse clings to wave-washed Gannet Rock at the entrance to the Bay of Fundy, about 10 kilometres (6 miles) southwest of Grand Manan. At high tide, a very small island of a few square metres of coarse conglomerate is all that shows above water. In times of storm, it is all awash. Loud were the predictions of imminent destruction when a sturdy wooden tower of massive hand-hewn timbers was erected there on a dressed stone base in 1831. After the lighthouse survived a wild gale in the winter of 1842, the authorities added a retaining wall, which was later jacketed in cement. The lighthouse has stood ever since, steadfast in one of the stormiest places on earth.

Now fully automated, the Gannet Rock lighthouse is alone in the sea with solar panels supplying power. Its two-ended, airport-type beacon shines from an octagonal aluminum lamphouse with flat panes of glass installed in 1967.

This old living lighthouse, with its tapering black and white vertically striped daymark, has outlived its gloomy critics by more than a century. It is unfortunate that wooden towers do not last forever, so on one sad day in the next few decades, this lighthouse will be replaced by a soulless steel tower. Perhaps the wonderful old tower, a monument to the planners and skilled craftsmen of long ago, could be moved intact to a site on the mainland.

Gannet Rock is accessible only by boat in fine weather, but landing is discouraged. On clear days, it is just visible as a speck on the sea from Southwest Head on Grand Manan Island.

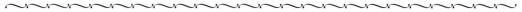

MACHIAS SEAL ISLAND

In 1832, a wooden lighthouse similar to the one on Gannet Rock was erected by Canadians on a low uninhabited rocky island in international waters some 19 kilometres (12 miles) southwest of Grand Manan. When the 5-kilometre (3-mile) limit in coastal waters was increased to 322 kilometres (200 miles) in 1977, its ownership was in doubt. After arbitration by the World Court and the redrawing of boundaries, the Machias Seal Island lighthouse now officially lies in Canadian territorial waters. Because of its controversial background, it is unlikely that this lighthouse will ever be anything but fully manned.

The first light was supplied by lamps with parabolic reflectors, but these were soon replaced by a much more effective single multiwick Argand lamp. The present reinforced concrete tower,

equipped with a Fresnel lens system, dates from 1915. Later, a bank of sealed beams on the earlier rotating base supplied its regular flashes for mariners journeying up the coast into the Bay of Fundy. At present, a large rotating double-ended bull's-eye searchlight is the beacon. The tower is festooned with aerials and an electronic foghorn array.

In the sea near the lighthouse's location and in adjacent waters at the mouth of the Bay of Fundy, the sea is full of fish attracted by cold nutrient-rich waters stirred by the tremendous tidal currents. The abundant fish attract several species of whales and seabirds, making Machias Seal Island a nesting place for thousands of terns, puffins, gannets, and guillemots. It is now a protected wildlife sanctuary. Bird-watchers arrive in summer on carefully scheduled trips from Grand Manan and Maine under supervision of the Canadian Wildlife Service.

Southwest Head (Grand Manan Island)

The Southwest Head lighthouse, as a complete station, was part of a spectacular scene as it sat on the edge of the 52-metre (171-foot) cliffs at the southwest end of Grand Manan Island. The present slightly lonesome looking short square tower on a single-storey square building still sends its beacon light out over the cliffs and jagged rocks on the approaches to the Bay of Fundy. The main body of Grand Manan lies to the north, and the American coast looms along the horizon to the northwest. Small dots in the sea mark Gannet Rock and Machias Seal Island with their lighthouses to the south.

Southwest Head is readily accessible by following the main road on Grand Manan, Route 776, south to its end at the lightstation. The lighthouse has a wonderful view with marvellous seascapes and an ocean full of marine life, including fish, whales, dolphins, and seabirds in the nutrient-rich waters stirred up by the visible currents generated by the tides of the Bay of Fundy, which can reach 16 metres (53 feet).

Grand Harbour ▲

An abandoned and disintegrating lighthouse has rested for many years on a rocky knoll in Grand Harbour, south of the mainland ferry landing on Grand Manan. Built in 1887, it was a white shingled tower about 9 metres (30 feet) tall with a substantial attached dwelling. It is visible from the wharf in Grand Harbour on the main road, Route 776. Interested citizens are attempting to raise money to preserve this piece of Grand Manan heritage before it disappears.

Great Duck Island ◀

Great Duck Island is among the northernmost of the several islands off the southeast side of Grand Manan. A white, square-based concrete service unit has a square tower with a lantern-house on one corner, which replaced an older wooden lighthouse built in 1887.

Though the lighthouse is accessible only by boat, it is visible from Whitehead Island, which is accessible from a road leading off Route 776 at Grand Harbour.

Swallowtail

Grand Manan Island is situated in the Bay of Fundy on the extreme southwest corner of New Brunswick at the boundary between Canada and the United States. It is a mecca for whale- and bird-watchers and for those wanting to enjoy spectacular marine scenery and a quiet pace of life. For many thousands of tourists each year, the Swallowtail lighthouse, at the ferry landing on the rocky point on the north side of North Head Harbour, is the point of welcome and farewell to many summer memories.

Constucted in 1860, its white octagonal tower stands about 16 metres (53 feet) high and is braced by cables that extend from anchors in the rock to just below the platform. The platform, oddly enough, has only seven sides due to an addition near the top of one of its sloping sides. Its red octagonal lamp-house with square flat glass panes houses the rotating beacon. At night, I have seen its flash from the New Brunswick shore near Pocologan, a distance of 40 kilometres (25 miles). I recall once looking for a good photo angle around the light when the keeper came out. A few minutes later, I was inside the keeper's house, sharing the family lunch of delicious fresh cod.

The Swallowtail lighthouse is easily accessible from the nearby North Head ferry landing, but the last kilometre (0.6 mile) must be travelled on foot. The old keeper's house is now a tearoom and Bed and Breakfast. Local residents are campaigning to rebuild and preserve this Grand Manan landmark.

Long Eddy Point ▲

Situated on the high basalt cliffs at the northeast corner of Grand Manan, the Long Eddy Point lighthouse looks west across the Grand Manan Channel to where the Canada–US border emerges between Campobello Island and the State of Maine. The widely known red-and-white striped West Quoddy light, on the most easterly point in the United States, complements Long Eddy Point to bracket the northern end of the Grand Manan Channel. The Canadian lighthouse takes its name from the powerful Fundy tidal currents that make a huge eddy below the point. The cold nutrient-rich Fundy water sustains a wealth of fish that sustain, in turn, whales and dolphins, sea gulls, and cormorants. The helicopter pad makes a wonderful observation platform for viewing the scene below.

The lightstation, a square building with a square concrete tower on one corner, is automated and on the local power grid. A flashing beacon with a red sector light on the landward side is about 38 metres (125 feet) above the sea and can be seen across the channel entrance and northward.

This lighthouse is readily accessible on the road leading northwest from North Head and the ferry terminal.

Southwest Wolf Island ▶

Southwest Wolf Island, about halfway between Grand Manan and Black's Harbour, is visible from the Grand Manan ferry. In 1982, a white cylindrical tower with an automatic flashing light replaced the older lighthouse tower. Though the view of the lighthouse from the ferry is distant, it is an excellent example of what most people envision as a remote lighthouse scene.

Head Harbour

The bright red St. George's cross on the white tower at Head Harbour, on Campobello Island, is one of the most widely known of Canada's several hundred lighthouses, appearing on calendars, in tourist literature, and in picture books. This daymark, as any other, helps mariners recognize a lighthouse tower against a white horizon or fogbank, or in the mist and drizzle of wet days. Other lights near Head Harbour also have notable daymarks, the most unusual being nearby West Quoddy Head in Maine, with its eight red and seven white stripes—a regular barber pole.

The Head Harbour lighthouse is one of the oldest wooden towers still in service in Canada. Construction started in 1829 and was completed in 1831. The lighthouse is almost 15 metres (49 feet) tall, and with its range of about 21 kilometres (11 nautical miles), it serves marine traffic at the entrance to Passamaquoddy Bay with the area's many islands, high tides, and tricky currents.

Campobello Island is accessible by causeway from highways in Maine, at Lubec, and from southern New Brunswick by ferry. Roads and footpaths lead to the island's northern tip, from where the small island on which the lightstation stands are visible. It is accessible for only two hours at low tide, and if visitors are stranded by the rapidly rising waters, they must wait eight hours until the causeway is passable again.

A decommissioned lighthouse at Mulholland Point, at the Campobello end of the bridge from Maine, is now part of Roosevelt Campobello International Park. It was built in 1885 and is 14 metres (46 feet) high. It no longer shows a light.

Letete Passage ▲

An octagonal light tower about 12 metres (39 feet) tall stands at the end of Green's Point, about 2 kilometres (1.25 miles) south of the Letete terminus of the Deer Island ferry. The first station was built in 1879, and the present tower, which guards the passage into Passamaquoddy Bay at the north end of Deer Island, was constructed in 1903. Decommissioned in 1999, it is now a museum and research station run by the Green's Point Lighthouse Association.

The Letete Passage lighthouse can be reached by taking the Letete Passage road off Highway 172, southwest of St. George, which is on Route 1. Though the lighthouse is no longer active, the foghorn still serves.

Beaver Harbour (Drew's Head) ▶

Beaver Harbour, a charming little fishing village, is reached by taking Highway 778 from Highway 1 near Pennfield. Seaward from the docks is the small, modern, cylindrical lighthouse on nearby Drew's Head.

The Beaver Harbour lighthouse can be reached on foot from the end of the road on a steep, stoney path.

POINT LEPREAU

In 1831, when the first keeper took up his duties in the new lighthouse on Point Lepreau, a few kilometres west of Saint John, his most complicated technological tasks had to do with maintaining the oil lamps and the turning mechanism for his light. He couldn't have dreamed that 150 years later a nuclear generating station would rise in the woods just behind his lighthouse and that, in a millisecond, it would generate vastly more energy than he could supply in a lifetime winding the clockwork weights to turn the light.

When first built, Point Lepreau was one of five lighthouses in the Bay of Fundy pointing the way to the increasingly busy port of Saint John. Its modern tower is a white concrete octagon some 18 metres (59 feet) high with a daymark of three horizontal red bands. By 1915, it had telephone service to enable the reporting of ship movements in the bay. It is now completely automated and stands with one small service building on the bare point.

From Highway 2, the Point Lepreau lighthouse can be reached by the road to the nuclear station, which passes beside the perimeter fence to the sea. Because of security concerns after September 11, 2001, this lighthouse is not accessible to visitors.

Pounding surf at Point Lepreau.

MUSQUASH HEAD

A reinforced concrete tower 14 metres (46 feet) tall and typical of lighthouse construction in Canada during the mid-20th century sits on Musquash Head, halfway between Point Lepreau and Saint John. It is recognizable by its white tower, single horizontal red band, and red cap. The Musquash Head lighthouse is part of the coastal aids system leading to one of Canada's major ports at Saint John. The original lighthouse on the station was built in 1879.

Musquash Head is accessible from Highway 2, along the coastal road loop through Lorneville, and a marked side road.

PARTRIDGE ISLAND

The Partridge Island lighthouse stands high above the entrance to Saint John Harbour and the mouth of the Saint John River. During the latter days of the American Revolution and the years following, shiploads of Loyalists came to Saint John and spread out over southern New Brunswick and up the river into the interior. By 1791, a lighthouse had been constructed on Partridge Island, but little is known of its history. The present 14-metre (46-foot) octagonal concrete tower dates from 1961 and is now entirely automated with an airport-type beacon. Its significant history and proximity to a major city make this lighthouse an ideal candidate for a national historic site and public park.

Brilliant red vertical stripes alternate with white on the tower's octagonal flanks, making a highly visible daymark in this especially foggy place. In 1932, I visited the earlier tower here, and keeper Lauder and my boyhood friend, his son, showed me the Fresnel lens and its clockwork mechanism with a mercury float. It was the first lighthouse I ever visited.

The discontinuing of the foghorn in 1998 was a sad historical event. Not that the electronic horn was any treat, but in 1860, Partridge Island was the scene of the first steam fog whistle with a clockwork mechanism to keep its signal regular in frequency and duration. In 1902, J.P. Northey of Toronto developed the diaphone horn wherein a horizontally pulsing piston produced a low note that carried for many kilometres over the sea. This Canadian invention spread rapidly throughout the world, and by 1904, Partridge Island had its own diaphone. I recall fondly my boyhood in this coastal city, when I grew used to hearing the Partridge Island "groaner" sending out its booming two-tone signal on foggy nights.

Now Partridge Island sends out its light in silence among the ruins of the old station. The few remaining houses have been boarded up or vandalized, immigration and quarantine hospitals have been mostly demolished, graveyards are overgrown with bushes, and various fortifications from a variety of wars are weathering away. A large Celtic cross stands on the island as a reminder of the hundreds of immigrants who died in quarantine here during the 18th and early 19th centuries.

The Partridge Island lighthouse is accessible only by boat or helicopter. It can, however, be viewed from the Digby ferry or with binoculars from the end of City Line (a street in West Saint John), and from Fort Dufferin, the nearest land.

Saint John Harbour

In 1980, Coast Guard staff built a small lighthouse on the end of their dock at the foot of King Street in the heart of downtown Saint John. Equipped with a light brought from Grindstone Island in the upper Bay of Fundy, it looks totally at home surrounded by ships, spars, buoys, and anchors.

The light is located inside the security fence of the Coast Guard base but is easily visible from the Market Slip area. It is accessible by taking the City Centre exit from Route 1 within the city.

Another small white lighthouse with a red top, which once stood at the Nova Scotia end of the Saint John–Digby ferry run, was decommissioned, moved across the bay, and reinstalled next to the old-fashioned Barbour's General Store at nearby Market Slip. It is well maintained and adds to the maritime scene at Market Slip, where history was made in the late 18th century with the arrival in New Brunswick of hundreds of Loyalists seeking safe haven from the American Revolution.

CAPE SPENCER ▲

For many years, a lightstation complete with keepers' houses marked Cape Spencer on the extreme eastern edge of the inlet leading into the port of Saint John. Now the only operating part is a modern automated beacon on a round fibreglass tower about 8 metres (26 feet) tall with a horizontal red and white pattern as a daymark. Old foundations mark the positions of earlier lights.

The lighthouse is accessed from Bayside Drive (past the huge dry-dock establishment in East Saint John), and then via Red Head Road past Mispec Beach. Along the way are many marine views, including Partridge Island and its lighthouse. This is a beautiful place on a fine day with the cliffs and shoreline of the Bay of Fundy just below and marine activity offshore.

SAINT JOHN RIVER ▶

Since the coming of the Loyalists in the latter half of the 18th century, the Saint John River has been a water highway into the interior of New Brunswick from the sea at Saint John. From the mid-1800s to the 1940s, steamboats regularly travelled the roughly 160 kilometres (100 miles) to Fredericton, or followed the Jemseg River into Grand Lake and on to Chipman. A series of landings and wharves marked the route at many places, and small lighthouses were provided to allow night travel.

One of my boyhood memories is being put on the boat by my grandfather at Chipman, and, after many stops, landing home a day later at Saint John with a load of agricultural produce for the city market. As children, we used to love to watch the plumes of black smoke from

The picturesque coastline near Cape Spencer.

the coal-burning boats *Majestic* and *D.J. Purdy* rising into the hills above Saint John as they started their runs upriver to Fredericton. Now only pleasure boats cruise the river in summer following the ghosts of the steamers and tugs towing booms of pulpwood or barges of chips or lumber.

Although the 1998 Canadian Coast Guard *List of Lights* notes some 41 buoys, spars, and skeleton towers remaining to guide summer traffic, few reminders remain from earlier days other than some of the concrete ramps and wharves, and a few lighthouses.

Green Head (or Swift Point) ◄

For more than a century, the Green Head lighthouse has provided a landmark for the entrance to the gorges of the Saint John River, just above the Reversing Falls. This landmark is a tapering four-sided white tower with a flaring platform base and the usual four-square lamphouse on top.

The Green Head lighthouse stands proudly as a reminder of times past and now acts only as a guide to pleasure boats in summer. Die-hard lighthouse enthusiasts can reach it by taking Exit 107 off Route 1 in Saint John West, travelling north on Catherwood, turning right on Manawagonish Road, and then left onto Church Street. At Green Head Road, turn right to Randolf and walk out the rough old quarry road about 1 kilometre (0.6 mile) to the lighthouse. A more distant view is available from Rivershore Road off Woodward Avenue in the Milledgeville district of Saint John.

Belyea's Point ►

A tapering pyramid with a hexagonal lamphouse some 11 metres (36 feet) high stands next to the beach at Belyea's Point on the north side of the southwest end of Long Reach on the Saint John River. It is a typical white wooden tower with a red-painted platform and a lamphouse with plain square glass windows. It is visible for many kilometres along Long Reach and the corner where the Saint John River changes from southwest to southeast.

Access is from Routes 7 or 177 from West Saint John, turning right onto Route 102 for about 3 kilometres (2 miles), and then turning right again down the Morrisdale Beach road.

Oak Point ▲

A lighthouse representative of earlier times remains at Oak Point near the northeast end of Long Reach on a beach along the northwest side of the river off Route 102. The area around it is the Kiwanis Oak Point Provincial Park.

The Oak Point lighthouse, a white square tower, stands on four concrete posts to avoid the freshet, as spring high water is called in these parts. Its light is housed in a simple square lamphouse with plain glass windows some 15 metres (49 feet) above the water.

Gagetown Ferry ◀

A cable ferry crosses the Saint John River at Gagetown on Route 102. At its western end, the Gagetown terminus, a small square boxlike lighthouse with a square red lanternhouse is mounted on timber stilts. It shows a winking yellow light. With the rerouting of the Trans-Canada Highway and a new bridge constructed nearby, the days of this lighthouse are probably numbered.

Access is from Route 102 following the ferry signs.

FREDERICTON

Recently, a large structure reminiscent of the traditional form of a lighthouse was constructed on the Saint John River front in the centre of Fredericton. Faintly vulgar to the aficionado of true lighthouses, it is several storeys high and fitted with elaborate outside fire escapes to serve the function of a public gathering place. It seems strange in its setting of buildings and monuments of genuine historical interest. Though it shows a useful light, it can only be described as an aberration because no lighthouse on the Saint John River ever looked like this or was constructed to serve as a public building.

Sand Point ▸

Two small lighthouses make an interesting day trip from Saint John. Both can be reached by heading north to Westfield on Route 7 or 177 from West Saint John, and turning off on the exit to Grand Bay. At Westfield, turn north on Route 177 to the ferry sign and take the short trip across the river to the Kingston Peninsula. Turn right on Route 845 and then right again on Sand Point Road to reach the strange sight of a small peppershaker lighthouse sitting atop a red steel frame tower at least twice its height. Lights such as these are seen in Canada at only a few places where small lights are needed high above very flat areas.

Bayswater ▲

Return to Route 845 and turn right toward the ferry at Bayswater. En route watch for another small peppershaker lighthouse, the archetypical Canadian wooden lighthouse, about 8 metres (26 feet) high. Little towers such as this were inexpensive and easy to build from local materials and had long life expectancy and simple maintenance requirements. In summer, the Bayswater light, with its small Fresnel lens, directs its flashing beam out over the Kingston Peninsula end of the Kennebecasis Bay ferry route to Milledgeville, a suburb of Saint John.

QUACO ▸

A white square tower on the corner of a white square building marks Quaco Head, just west of St. Martin's, some 40 kilometres (25 miles) east of Saint John. A lightstation was established here as early as 1837, at the beginning of the great boom in wooden shipbuilding at ports along the Fundy coast. This lasted well into the 20th century, when steel replaced wood and steamships took the place of commercial sailing vessels on the sea.

The Quaco lightstation is easily accessible by turning off Route 111 at West Quaco.

ST. MARTIN'S HARBOUR ▴

If you journey to Quaco, you may enjoy an excursion into St. Martin's, where a replica of a small lighthouse is located at the head of the harbour. Though nonfunctioning, it provides a classic example of a mid-19th century multisided lighthouse. The old lamphouse, large enough to accommodate rotating oil lamps and a lens, was at one time on the Quaco Head light. The two covered bridges within a few metres and the view of the small harbour to the sea make this an interesting and scenic destination. The lighthouse is a small museum with plaques on the grounds to recount the history of this once-active shipping and shipbuilding site.

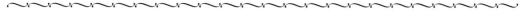

Cape Enragé

At many places in Canada, people have joined together to preserve local lighthouses as they are taken out of service. In the early 1990s, the Cape Enragé lightstation was scheduled for automation and demolition of most of its buildings, but it was saved by a group of students and their teacher from Moncton. Since then, the lighthouse has been lovingly restored to its former glory, and it is now operated by a group of volunteers, a testimony to their regard for their heritage.

The Cape Enragé lightstation dates from 1848, when a beacon was established to mark the entrance to Chignecto Bay and the top of the Bay of Fundy. About 15 kilometres (9 miles) from Alma and Fundy National Park, it is a scenic spot with sea cliffs about 65 metres (213 feet) high. The lighthouse is a sturdy peppershaker about 8 metres (26 feet) tall with a wide platform surmounted by an old-style hexagonal lamphouse. The foghorn apparatus and the light are open to visitors, and the keeper's residence and the service buildings now house a tearoom and gift shop. The original foundation is visible nearby.

With its proximity to the national park and its picturesque setting, this is a popular destination. It is reached from Route 114, east of Alma and Fundy National Park, on marked side roads.

East Coast to
Miramichi and Bay Chaleur

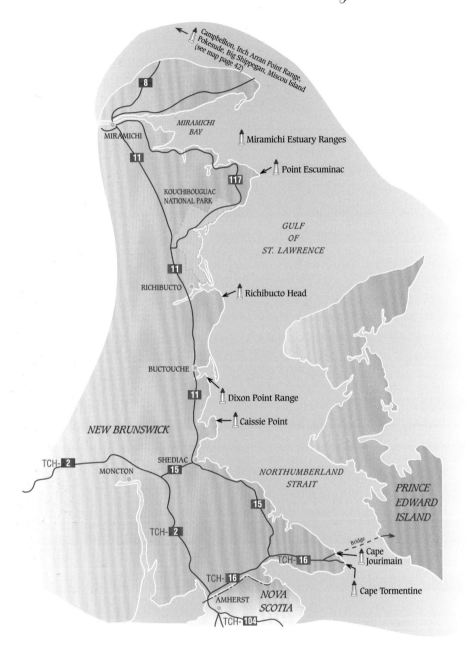

Campbellton, Inch Arran Point Range, Pokesudie, Big Shippegan, Miscou Island (see map page 42)

8

MIRAMICHI
BAY

MIRAMICHI

11

Miramichi Estuary Ranges

117

Point Escuminac

KOUCHIBOUGUAC
NATIONAL PARK

GULF
OF
ST. LAWRENCE

11

RICHIBUCTO

Richibucto Head

BUCTOUCHE

11

Dixon Point Range

Caissie Point

NEW BRUNSWICK

TCH- **2**

MONCTON

SHEDIAC

15

NORTHUMBERLAND
STRAIT

15

PRINCE
EDWARD
ISLAND

TCH- **2**

Bridge

Cape
Jourimain

TCH- **16**

TCH- **16**

Cape Tormentine

AMHERST

NOVA
SCOTIA

TCH- **104**

*I*n contrast to the deep water and
rocky shoreline along New Brunswick's south shore, the east coast is low-lying with extensive
sandbars and a number of drowned river valleys that form estuaries. The southern half of this area
is served by lighthouses here and there along the shoreline and also by lights on the
southwest side of Prince Edward Island.

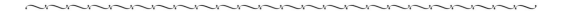

CAPE TORMENTINE

Completed in 1998, the Confederation Bridge across the Northumberland Strait between New Brunswick and Prince Edward Island is one of the great engineering feats in Canadian history. As soon as the bridge was opened, ferry service between Cape Tormentine, New Brunswick, and Borden, Prince Edward Island, effectively came to an end.

In this photograph taken before bridge construction, the ferry *Abegweit II* pushes through the springtime ice floes beyond the little lighthouse at the end of the Cape Tormentine pier. Over the years, many ships served on this lifeline for Prince Edward Island, but the original *Abegweit* was probably the most dear to islanders, who remember her battling across the strait in foul weather and through winter ice to maintain the link to "over there." Cape Tormentine, with its pier and little lighthouse, now orphans of progress, are accessible by turning off Route 16 east of the Confederation Bridge and following the signs.

CAPE JOURIMAIN

A lovely old wooden lighthouse some 16 metres (53 feet) high stands on a point just east of the New Brunswick end of the Confederation Bridge to Prince Edward Island, on what used to be an island in the midst of swamps and lagoons. The lighthouse was visible to passengers on the ferries that once operated from nearby Cape Tormentine across Northumberland Strait. Now standing alone and mute, it can be seen from the New Brunswick end of the bridge. The area around it has been set aside as a wildlife refuge with an interpretive centre and nature trails. An impressive view of the old Cape Jourimain light is possible from the beach at the end of the bridge as well as from an observation tower in the reserve itself.

The octagonal wooden tower tapers upward to a collar of nicely finished woodwork. There, what looks like an old lantern platform gives way to another 3 metres (10 feet) of tapering tower with fancy scrolled supports to the platform with its plain wooden balustrade. A ten-sided lanternhouse with flat square panes is capped with a mushroom-shaped vent for its original oil lamps.

The Cape Jourimain lighthouse is the victim of different lines of progress: the automation of lighthouses generally and the brightly lit bridge specifically, itself a giant lighthouse visible for many kilometres along the strait. At the New Brunswick end of the bridge, exits now lead to a major tourist centre. A fee is charged for access to the interpretive centre and ecological reserve, where trails through woods and wetlands lead to the lighthouse.

Caissie Point

A well-maintained lighthouse tower, recognized as a heritage structure, is located on a peninsula north of Shediac at Caissie Point. The white wooden tower about 12 metres (39 feet) tall and decked out in red trim stands alone now, the attached dwelling and residence having been removed. Its octagonal lantern-house of the traditional pattern shows an intermittent yellow light.

Turn off Route 11 at Exit 7 for Grande Digue, and then onto Route 530 to Caissie Point. The lighthouse is visible from Route 530 and is located at the water's edge down a short entrance road. Permission to cross private property should be requested.

DIXON POINT RANGE

Two neat, pyramidal white wooden towers with red tops and bright red vertical stripes mark Dixon Point on New Brunswick's Buctouche shore. They are a good example of paired range lights.

Access to the Dixon Point range lights is from the Route 535, along the coast at St. Thomas, south of Buctouche.

Richibucto Head ▲

A white wooden tower with a red top now stands alone, where once there was a full lightstation with a residence and a service building.

The Richibucto Head lighthouse is adjacent to Route 505 near Cap-Lumière. It looks out over the northwest end of the Northumberland Strait.

Point Escuminac ◀

In 1841, a lighthouse was established on Point Escuminac on the southeast corner of the outside entrance to Miramichi Bay. After several changes of tower and lamp, it become a slender white reinforced concrete hexagon with its airport beacon in 1962. Each of its six sides flares out at the top to make a cement platform with red railings and an octagonal lamphouse with flat glass panes. Its bank of electronic horns and its small service buildings stand with the tower on the low shoreline facing the Gulf of St. Lawrence, more or less directly across from North Cape, at the tip of Prince Edward Island.

To reach the Point Escuminac lighthouse, drive down a small side road along the shore from Escuminac village on Route 117, east of Miramichi.

MIRAMICHI ESTUARY RANGES

Low sandy islands, spits, and shoals mark the broad east side of Miramichi Bay on New Brunswick's east coast. The channels through the very low islands and spits across the east side of Miramichi Bay require range lights that can be seen for many kilometres. Small lighthouses on steel stilts mark some of these, such as Fox and Portage islands. Other markers are on piles. One at Grand Dune is a caisson surrounded by water. Its cylindrical steel base was sunk into the sand and then filled with stone and gravel. It now displays a small pole light and a white daymark with a red vertical stripe on the seaward side. These lighthouses are accessible only by water.

The Grand Dune caisson under construction in 1980.

POKESUDIE ▶

Archives recount a story of a white square tower that stood at Pokesudie on the coastal flats north of Miramichi Bay for about 80 years from the 1890s. This photograph from the early 1970s is thought to be this tower. It is not listed in the most recent Canadian Coast Guard *List of Lights*. (*Location marked on map of St. Lawrence River Lower North Shore on page 42.*)

BIG SHIPPEGAN ▼

In 1872, an octagonal wooden tower 12 metres (39 feet) high with a red lamphouse was placed on a sandbar at the east side of Shippegan Gully (*Gully* meaning "harbour entry"). Its neat shingled sides taper to a well-crafted flare at the wooden platform and a red railing with an affixed emergency light. Its round lamphouse with a red roof, curved glass panes, spherical cap, and weather vane is typical of the Barbier-manufactured tops of the time. Its base is unusual in that the precisely shingled sides end about a metre (3.3 feet) above the ground, revealing concrete posts set into the sand on each corner and at the centre.

The Big Shippegan lighthouse is accessible along a local road from Shippegan, itself reached on Route 113, which leaves the main Route 11 between Pokemouche and Haut Pokemouche. (*Location marked on map of St. Lawrence River Lower North Shore on page 42.*)

Tall range light in Shippegan Gully area.

Big Shippegan.

Miscou Island ▶

A major lighthouse was placed on Miscou Island, at the extreme northeast tip of New Brunswick, to mark the southeast side of the entrance to Chaleur Bay. The octagonal tower was built of hand-hewn timbers, clad in wood, and shingled. Originally 23 metres (76 feet) high, it was extended to 25 metres (82 feet) in 1903. Early in its history, it was equipped with a Fresnel lens system and diaphone, indicators of its functions as a major coastal light. The land is low at Shippegan and Miscou Island, so lights are especially important for those at sea.

The Miscou Island lighthouse is accessible from Route 113, which joins the main coastal road, Route 11. *(Location marked on map of St. Lawrence River Lower North Shore on page 42.)*

Lighthouse lovers will not want to witness what has happened to a lighthouse at Grand Anse, off Route 11 on the south side of Chaleur Bay, west of Caraquet. The pristine old white tower with its red cap has been spoiled with a maudlin paint scheme consisting of horizontal layers of red, white, and blue in equal proportions, and marked with an Acadian star. In tourist literature photographs, it resembles a caricature of an actual lighthouse.

Inch Arran Point Range ▲

A unique lighthouse stands at the eastern end of Victoria Street in Dalhousie, adjacent to a city park. A tapering square wooden tower some 10 metres (33 feet) high holds an octagonal lamphouse with an unusual set of thin railings that extend in a sort of a birdcage all the way up to the gutters of the dome. This odd feature is designed to prevent gulls from nesting. The clearly visible lens is a fixed Fresnel type with an electric light giving a flash every few seconds to form the front of the range. The back marker with its red-striped daymark is visible through the trees to the west.

The main tower is white, but its door, windows, platform supports, railings and trim are painted Coast Guard red with white maple leaves added. *(Location marked on map of St. Lawrence River Lower North Shore on page 42.)*

CAMPBELLTON

A beautifully maintained residence and lighthouse tower enclosed in a white fence with neat grounds are located beside the waterfront driveway in Campbellton, on the shore of Bay Chaleur.

Officially called the Campbellton Rear Range, it was a simple steel tower until recently when the Town of Campbellton built a 16-metre (53-foot) tower around it. The residence beside it now operates as a hostel. The new tower is a fairly massive tapering octagon with a red top, a somewhat flattened lanternhouse, and a red stripe on the seaward side as a daymark. It is a splendid example of an otherwise undistinguished range light becoming a town landmark. *(Location marked on map of St. Lawrence River Lower North Shore on page 42.)*

Panmure Island, Prince Edward Island.

Lighthouses
of
Prince Edward
Island

The north side of Prince Edward Island fronts the open waters of the Gulf of St. Lawrence along a shallow and much indented shoreline with long offshore sandbars and beautiful beaches. The south side of the island faces the warm sheltered waters of the Northumberland Strait in a series of low cliffs of red sandstone and shale, alternating with long beaches and reddish sandbars. For centuries, fleets of fishing boats have sailed out from sheltered places along this coast—places located in drowned stream valleys, in small artificial harbours, and through breaks in long offshore sandbars. All of these refuges have been marked with local harbour lights, range lights, and channel markers.

In the mid-19th century, major lighthouses were built to guide ships in the Gulf of St. Lawrence at East End Point and at Cape North, and in the Northumberland Strait, where a series of lighthouses dots the coast from Souris in the east to West Point. Most of these are superbly constructed wooden structures proudly maintained by islanders. Prince Edward Island is probably the only place in Canada where you will find lighthouses in the middle of lush potato fields.

Range lights are aids for entering bays, inlets, and harbours, and they typically consist of an outer light on a point, island, or shoal and an inner light, usually much higher and set back as much as 1,000 metres (3,280 feet). In daylight, these markers are useful, but at night they are essential to guiding mariners, who visually align these lights to know the safe points of entry into narrow waterways. Prince Edward Island has several unusual range lights with some of the back lights famous for their tall, skinny, even awkward shapes.

Lighthouses are an important part of Prince Edward Island tourism. As they became destaffed and automated, many have been taken over by local societies of interested citizens. Activities around the old lights range from care and preservation to operating a bed and breakfast and museum. If you plan to travel from one end of Prince Edward Island to the other, pick up a ribbon at either the East Point or North Cape lighthouses and present it at the other end for a Traveller's Certificate.

Lighthouses of Prince Edward Island

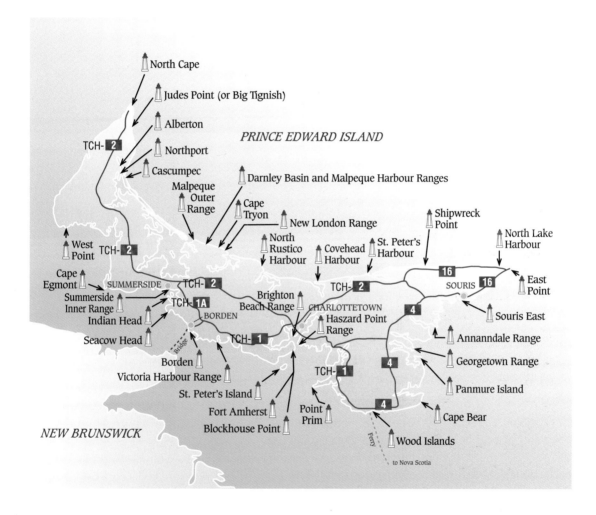

*P*rince Edward Island is Canada's
smallest province. Distances between destinations are short, so you can
begin a tour of lighthouses from almost any point. Since access to the province
is either via the Confederation Bridge from Cape Tormentine, New
Brunswick, to Borden, Prince Edward Island, or via the ferry
from Caribou, Nova Scotia, to Wood Islands, Prince
Edward Island, the sequence in this book starts at
Charlottetown and goes each direction
around the island.

Charlottetown East to Central North Shore

Brighton Beach Range Lights ▲ ▶

The Trans-Canada Highway, Route 1, goes through downtown Charlottetown on University Avenue. In the downtown, turn west onto Euston Street and drive eight blocks to Queen Elizabeth Drive, a lovely waterside street that overlooks the harbour and includes two interesting lighthouses officially known as the Brighton Beach range lights.

The front range light's red cap sits on a tapering square tower resting on a concrete base with its feet in the water. Visitors can walk down to it on a side street that leads to the water's edge.

A little farther along to the north is the back range light, an unusual, tall hexagonal column that flares out to a round platform. A similar Coast Guard tower design is found in a few other places, but this one is unique in that its light peers out from under the platform instead of being mounted on top. Since this photograph was taken in about 1980, its daymark has been altered from horizontal red bands to a vertical red stripe. Recently, the whole area has been built up, so the seaward view is no longer accessible.

Haszard Point Range ◀

Haszard Point, on the east side of the entrance to Charlottetown Harbour, is blessed with a back range light that is much photographed for its unusual shape and size. This tall wooden structure, built in 1889, tapers upward from its square base for about half its height, then tapers more gently to a lightly constructed platform with a red railing. The square red lamphouse with its plain glass window faces the sea. Its daymark is described in the Canadian Coast Guard *List of Lights* as a red vertical stripe, but earlier photographs show an orange diamond. In the 1998 Canadian Coast Guard *List of Lights*, it is described as a red tower with a black vertical stripe. It must mark an unusual peril to be spelled "haszard."

Access is off the Trans-Canada Highway, Route 1, at the east end of the main bridge over the Hillsborough River. Go through the suburb of Stratford and south to the shore road (1A) to the east side of the harbour entrance.

Fort Amherst ▶

The Fort Amherst light is one of two modest peppershaker wooden lighthouses located at the Fort Amherst National Historic Site, on the west side of the entrance to Charlottetown Harbour. Together these lighthouses are sometimes referred to as the Warren Cove range lights.

These lights may be reached by taking the Trans-Canada Highway west of Charlottetown and following Route 19 south from Cornwall. The light is on the west side of the entrance to Charlottetown Harbour. Lately, a gaudy red stripe has been painted from the front steps all the way to the lantern top, including the front door and the window.

Blockhouse Point ▲

Even among the many beautifully constructed wooden lighthouses on Prince Edward Island, the lighthouse on Blockhouse Point is outstanding. It was a combined residence and tower with superbly crafted windows, doors, and cornices, even on the base of the platform. The light tower is square, 12 metres (39 feet) high, with an octagonal lanternhouse and an omnidirectional lens. Its electric light gives a three-second flash with a one-second eclipse—more a winker than a flasher. The light is automated, and the residence is now privately occupied.

The Blockhouse Point lighthouse is accessible from the coastal road, Route 19, on the west side of the entrance to Charlottetown Harbour.

Point Prim

Point Prim is the oldest and perhaps the most beautiful lighthouse on Prince Edward Island. It has stood since 1846 on the point at the southeast side of Hillsborough Bay, on the outer approaches to Charlottetown Harbour. Its tapering round white tower, some 18 metres (59 feet) tall, is capped with a twelve-sided platform supported by graceful brackets. Its multisided red lanternhouse with tall rectangular panes of glass is capped by a wind-directed vent. Supporting rods from its roofline to its railing stanchions prevent seabirds from nesting. The tower's original round brick core was sheathed in wood and shingled in an unusually fine display of the carpenter's art.

Inside, four flights of stairs with four landings and inset windows lead to the electric light in the lanternhouse. An electric motor hums away as it rotates the Fresnel lens system, while remnants of the original clockwork mechanism stand by, reminders of the days when keepers climbed to the top every four hours to rewind the heavy system of weights.

Still largely in its original condition, the Point Prim lighthouse was completely automated by 1976, and the support buildings were removed. Now the centre of an historic site, it stands alone in a commanding location overlooking the red Prince Edward Island shoreline below. It is readily accessible on local road 209, leading off Route 1, east of Charlottetown. This location is truly a beautiful sight to lovers of lighthouses.

Wood Islands

Three lights mark the way for local traffic and the Nova Scotia ferry at Wood Islands, on the edge of the southern bulge of the east end of Prince Edward Island. Two of these are range lights for the ferry dock, including one saucy little fellow on the end of the pier.

The third, on the south side of the east portion of the larger island, is a substantial tapering white tower about 15 metres (49 feet) high rising from a corner of the residence house. The six-sided red lanternhouse is of the old style with plain sheets of glass. Its windows and trim are picked out in Coast Guard red, as are the residence roof and windows. This lighthouse, now part of Wood Islands Provincial Park, is operated by a local community group and is open to visitors in the summer.

The route to the ferry is conspicuously marked. Follow the main road, Route 1, from Charlottetown. Once at the terminal, watch for an exit to the left that stays outside the ferry entrance and goes on to the main lights.

CAPE BEAR

A white square tower 12 metres (39 feet) high with a small service annex stands on Cape Bear just southeast of Murray Harbour, on the southeast corner of Prince Edward Island. Three levels of windows lead to the platform and a traditional octagonal lanternhouse with a small ventilator on top. A railed balcony at ground level provides a viewing platform for the marine scenery of the eastern end of the Northumberland Strait and across toward Cape Breton.

This is a very pleasant stopping place. It is accessible from the coastal road, Route 18. A well-marked side road leads directly to the parking lot at the lighthouse.

Panmure Island

Panmure Island, on the east side of Prince Edward Island, is tied to the Prince Edward Island mainland by a splendid long beach and sandbar, now a provincial park. It is a marker for the south side of Georgetown Harbour and bears a major lighthouse on its outer edge that is a fine example of the beautifully designed wooden towers characteristic of the island. Built in 1853, it stands about 18 metres (59 feet) high.

Its massive tapering octagonal tower is capped with a matching platform supported by scrolled wooden brackets. Neatly framed windows mark the four interior levels. Its rotating lens system is housed in a ten-sided lamphouse that is typical of lighthouses built at the time when oil lamps needed considerable space. The large wind-controlled vent on the very top is further evidence of its former fuel-burning lamp days. Bird prevention rods lead from the stanchions of the plain railing to the edge of the roof. The lantern windows are especially tall rectangles of plain glass. Its interior shows massive hand-hewn timbers for the main frames. The wood sheathing is finished with neat shingling that was replaced in 1956 after long service. With automation and destaffing, the former residence is now privately occupied, and many of the tall trees that used to grace the grounds have disappeared.

The Panmure Island lighthouse is a handsome sight on its headland as it is approached along the beach sandbar. A must-see for any serious lighthouse aficionado, it is accessible from Montague or Murray River on Route 17 and then by following Route 347 through Panmure Island Provincial Park.

Georgetown Range ▲

Once past Panmure Island, lighthouse mariners en route to Georgetown Harbour were aided by range lights. The back range is 12 metres (39 feet) high and square with white sides tapering to a square platform and a broad red band on the seaward side for a daymark. The usual plain lanternhouse with plain glass windows shows a small fixed light.

The Georgetown range light is accessible on a side road, Lower Montague Road, off Route 17 east of Montague.

Annanndale Range ▶

An unusually tall slender range light is located at Annanndale, accessible from the main Route 4 at Dundas via Route 310, and a side road to the right to Annanndale Wharf, just southwest of Little Pond.

Souris East

A major light serves Souris Harbour for local marine traffic and the ferry to the Magdalen Islands. It is a tapering square tower about 14 metres (46 feet) high with a square platform supported by scrolled wooden brackets. The top is a severe-looking round red lanternhouse with ventilation cap, which once housed a rotating Fresnel lens (above). Long since automated, mainland power now drives a bull's-eye–type light and a bank of electronic horns.

The lighthouse is accessible from Souris on a small side road off coastal Route 16.

East Point ▶

The easternmost tip of Prince Edward Island saw its first lighthouse in 1867, when a classic wooden tower some 20 metres (66 feet) high was placed less than a kilometre (0.6 mile) away from the edge of the point. When HMS *Phoenix* sank on a nearby offshore reef in 1882, part of the blame was attached to the location of the lighthouse, which was said to be too far back from the hazards. The whole structure was moved much closer to the dangerous shore. Some 25 years later, erosion threatened the tower, so it was moved again, this time about 60 metres (197 feet) back to its present position. Its survival of two moves is a testimony to its builders' solid construction methods. Eroding cliffs and retreating lights have long been part of the island scene, the latest being the relocation of the Cape Egmont lighthouse back from its cliff-front location in 1998.

The East Point lighthouse is a classic wooden structure of the mid-19th century. Inside, massive timbers with diagonal braces form the corners of the tapering octagonal tower. The outside is heavy planking with shingles up to the flare below the wooden platform, which has an ornate railing around its red deck. The red ten-sided lanternhouse still houses a perfectly preserved rotating catoptric light system, which has seen a long evolution from oil lamps to the electric light of today. Its first foghorn was installed in 1885 at the time of its first move. Now the station is automated with radar sensors and a bank of electronic foghorns.

With its lighthouse duties completely automated, the keeperless station is now preserved and operated as a tourist attraction by a local group. It is accessible by a side road leading northeast from the main coastal road, Route 16, at the east end of Prince Edward Island.

North Lake Harbour ◀

About 10 kilometres (6 miles) along coastal Route 16 from the East End turnoff is a small inlet from the open sea that forms North Lake Harbour port. The range lights here are of interest only for demonstrating typical examples of the lights in small ports along the Prince Edward Island coast.

SHIPWRECK POINT ▲

A lighthouse tower about 14 metres (46 feet) tall stands at the village of Shipwreck Point, just off the coastal highway, Route 16, on the north side of Prince Edward Island. *Naufrage* is an alternate name for the port and lighthouse. This is an interesting little port with its lighthouse to one side in a grassy field above red sea cliffs with the gulf beyond and fishing boats coming and going.

The Shipwreck Point lighthouse is readily visible from the village centre, but care must be taken about crossing private property to visit it.

ST. PETER'S HARBOUR ▶

A tapering square white tower marks the west side of the entrance to St. Peter's Bay, on the north shore of Prince Edward Island. It is set amidst grassed and bare dunes with an old wharf nearby at the water's edge. The shoreline on the east side opposite the lighthouse is now part of Prince Edward Island National Park. The shifting sands over the years caused the harbour to silt up, resulting in its closing. The lighthouse now acts only as a coastal warning light.

From Charlottetown or from the east, the lighthouse is accessible via the main road, Route 2, from Morell, by small side roads marked St. Peter's Harbour, and then walking in from the end of the road. Use the power line that leads to the light as a guide.

Charlottetown West to Central North Shore

St. Peter's Island

St. Peter's Island lies offshore of Rice Point, a few nautical miles south of the entrance to Charlottetown Harbour. A modest lighthouse tower about 9 metres (30 feet) tall stands alone a few metres back from eroding cliffs of typical red Prince Edward Island sandstone on the southeast corner of the island. The top portion is now painted in Coast Guard red.

All supporting buildings of the former station have been removed, and the automated lighthouse carries out the duties of assisting ships in the Northumberland Strait.

The lighthouse is accessible only by boat.

VICTORIA HARBOUR RANGE

Several range lights are visible from the end of the bridge where Trans-Canada, Route 1, crosses Victoria Harbour on the south side of Prince Edward Island, about halfway between Charlottetown and Summerside. The back range light, built in 1878, is a standard tapering square tower with a square wooden platform, an octagonal lamphouse, and a wind-controlled vent on top. Its daymark used to be a bright red diamond on its white front, but now it is a more prosaic red vertical stripe. Two other range lights can be seen in Victoria Harbour.

BORDEN

The mighty Confederation Bridge, one the great engineering feats in Canada, spans the Northumberland Strait and ends at Borden, Prince Edward Island. When completed on May 31, 1997, the structure became the world's longest bridge over ice-covered waters. Engineers had to solve problems associated with drifting ice in winter while minimizing ecological impact. The bridge brought many changes to island life, including displacing the ferry system to New Brunswick that had served the island for more than a century. Borden was the ferry terminus on the island side.

The old ferry docks, complete with lighthouses, are located near the end of the bridge.

Near the end of the bridge, a tall, slender white range light (above) sits in a parklike setting. It is a typical Prince Edward Island range light in its tapering shingled exterior and modest lanternhouse with square plain glass windows. Preserved as part of local history, it marks progress in the end of the ferries and the modern bridge that dominates the scene.

The lighthouse on Port Borden Pier (left) is an upward-tapering hexagonal wooden structure with a railed platform supported by a dozen triangular brackets. On one side, a solar panel collects the energy to run the small light inside the square-windowed hexagonal lamphouse. The lighthouse is on the end of the pier, which has massive wave barriers on its seaward side.

This lighthouse is easily accessible. Park in the welcome village at the end of the bridge and walk out onto the pier. While a little forlorn in abandonment, it is well worth a visit, particularly for those with a sense of history. Its future is probably precarious unless preservationists take up the cause.

SEACOW HEAD

Seacow Head, located on the extreme southeast side of the entrance to Bedeque Bay and Summerside Harbour, is one of a series of lights along the Northumberland Strait side of Prince Edward Island. Built in 1863, its octagonal 18-metre (59-foot) wooden tower is another of the classic Prince Edward Island towers. The tapered octagonal exterior is white and shingled. The tower is capped by a platform with red railings that supports a red ten-sided lanternhouse with tall flat glass panes. Inside, heavy hand-hewn timbers are evident, and three iron rods across each of its three levels serve as braces. Its imported stone foundations are set into the soft red island rocks well below ground level.

Seacow Head is readily accessible off Route 1A east of Summerside. Then follow Routes 171, 112, and 119 in succession leading southwest from Central Bedeque.

INDIAN HEAD

A casual glance from the main road into Summerside from Borden rewards visitors with the sight of a small white finger at the end of a sandbar on the south side of the bay. This turns out to be an unusual lighthouse.

When I arrived on a late summer afternoon, it was nearly high tide. Swimmers enjoying the warm salt water splashing through the breakwater advised me that the lighthouse could be reached on foot at low tide, which would come next day at just after noon. Sure enough, when I returned it was easily walkable with only a few centimetres of water to be waded through at the far end.

Great blocks of khaki sandstone from Wallace, Nova Scotia, create a breakwater about 0.5 kilometre (0.3 mile) long. At its end sits an octagonal main house, tower and lamphouse rising from a concrete base in the mud. This unusual light, built in 1881, originally used the oil lamps typical of the time and was staffed by a resident

keeper. It has long since been electrified and automated with an omnidirectional Fresnel lens providing a five-second electric flash followed by a five-second eclipse.

The Indian Head lighthouse is a real gem in an accessible and picturesque spot. Take Route 171 southwest from Central Bedeque on Route 1A. Turn right onto Route 112 and continue past the end of the pavement to the end of the gravel. After a short distance along a pure red typical Prince Edward Island dirt road, you emerge on a grassy point with a beautiful view of the sea and coast.

SUMMERSIDE INNER RANGE ▶

Tall and ungainly, with wire braces to brace it against winds, the Summerside Inner Range is easily visible from a side street in downtown Summerside. From the sea, it appears as a white finger with a red stripe on its seaward side, showing a steady light. Built in 1895, the square tower tapers from its base upward for about 12 metres (39 feet). The square straight-sided upper tower supports a lightly built railed platform and a square single-windowed lamp-house. Its companion range lights are along the seaward shore.

CAPE EGMONT ▲

The tiny artificial harbour of Cape Egmont is home port to some fishermen on Northumberland Strait. Nearby sits the Cape Egmont lighthouse, built in 1884 on a cliff of typically red Prince Edward Island sandstone and shale. The station is entirely automated with power coming from the main grid. The old keepers' dwellings and service houses have been removed, and now only a radio tower with a small service building keep the lighthouse company. In 1998, erosion forced the Coast Guard to move the tower back from the 10-metre (33-foot) cliffs. A plaque on the side of the tower explains its history.

Cape Egmont is easily accessible from the coastal road, Route 11, west of Summerside.

West Point

The aptly named West Point marks the location where Prince Edward Island's Northumberland Strait shoreline turns from east–west to south–north toward North Cape at the very end of the island. The lighthouse is a classic Prince Edward Island wooden tower, although square in cross section instead of the usual hexagon or octagon. Heavy internal timbers frame the sloping sides with planking and shingles on the exterior. Straight flights of stairs bring visitors up three levels onto the platform, where the original twelve-sided cast-iron lamphouse still holds its red top some 20 metres (66 feet) above the ground. Twelve tall rectangles of plain glass house the beacon, which burned oil until electrified in 1963. Its railed platform is the characteristic Prince Edward Island wooden pattern with support brackets beneath. It still shows a light.

Tourist literature often features the West Point lighthouse because of its bold daymark—three broad black horizontal stripes—uncommon on Canadian lights. It is located just back of a popular beach that is part of Cedar Dunes Provincial Park.

When automation left the lighthouse abandoned, a local community group built an addition to replace the old dwelling, and in 1988 converted this historic lighthouse station into an inn and restaurant. Its rooms house museum artifacts from island lighthouses. Local lore would have us believe that Captain Kidd buried some of his treasure in the sand dunes north of the lighthouse. Visitors to this readily accessible tower are invited to watch at night for a mysterious burning ghost ship offshore.

Take Route 2 to Carleton, then head south on Route 14. A well-marked short side road leads to Cedar Dunes Provincial Park and the lighthouse. It is a beautiful place amid sand dunes and beaches with salt water warm enough for swimming.

NORTH CAPE

A principal warning light in the western Gulf of St. Lawrence stands in a grassy field just back of North Cape on the northwest tip of Prince Edward Island. This superb wooden lighthouse was built in 1866 in the best Prince Edward Island tradition of fine craftsmanship. As erosion progressed on the point, the lighthouse was moved back more than once. Until recently, it stood alone, but it now shares the point with a communications tower several times as tall and a nearby cluster of experimental wind turbines. An interpretation centre and a restaurant are located nearby.

The tower's smoothly tapering octagonal shingled walls lead to an ornate wooden railing on its platform with a twelve-sided red lamphouse and a dome with a wind-directed ventilation funnel. It is about 18 metres (59 feet) high with a dioptric lens system and an electric light installed in 1970. Its beacon, some 25 metres (82 feet) above the sea, is visible from about 29 kilometres (18 miles) out to sea. In recent years, its doors, windows, and trim have been painted Coast Guard red, contrasting sharply with its white shingles.

Follow Route 2 west and north to Tignish, then take Route 12, the shore road, to North Cape.

Jude's Point (or Big Tignish)

The tourist road map of Prince Edward Island shows a lighthouse at Jude's Point on the Gulf of St. Lawrence, high up on the North Cape end of the island and east of Tignish. Exploration of that area in 2002 found that few locals knew about this lighthouse, but eventually the search led to the grounds of the Royal Star Foods plant in sight of the shore road, Route 12. A road just before the food plant leads to an abandoned sad-looking lighthouse.

The Jude's Point lighthouse is not listed in the 1998 *List of Lights*, so it must have been defunct for some time. It is a tapering four-sided faded white tower about 9 metres (30 feet) tall with a faded red hexagonal lamphouse and a large ventilator at the apex for the oil lamps of earlier times. It stands in a picturesque setting with a protected shore on the seaward side and a dredged channel leading into a long narrow harbour filled in season with fishing boats coming and going.

CASCUMPEC

The northern shore of Prince Edward Island is lined with long sandbars across the principal bays with occasional openings allowing fishing boats access to the inner waters. One of these sandbars is Cascumpec Island. Its northern end, marking the entry into Cascumpec Bay and Alberton, bears two lighthouses side by side. The old lighthouse, with its attached residence, has long been out of service and is now a private cottage. Not far from it, a skeleton tower with an enclosed interior column and a daymark of horizontal red bands bears the working light some 18 metres (59 feet) above the sea.

Take Route 150 off the main Route 2 to Alberton and then follow the road leading southeast to Northport. These lights are visible across the water from several places along the road and from the dock at Northport. Though distant, the view of the two lighthouses on the low island is most impressive.

Northport ▶

A white tower about 6 metres (20 feet) tall stands in an open area in front of the community hall at Northport, just beyond the docks. This is the rear Northport range light. Its front partner sits seaward on the end of the nearby wharf. From there the Cascumpec lights are visible out to sea.

Take Route 150 off the main Route 2 to Alberton and then follow the road leading southeast to Northport.

Alberton ▼

Small routine range lights and aids to navigation, typical of those all over the Atlantic provinces, are found leading to and inside the bays and harbours inside the long offshore bars in the Alberton area of Prince Edward Island. They may look like the small lighthouse-like structures, such as the example of Malpeque *(see page 121)*, or they may resemble the frame and shield structures such as North Lake Harbour *(see page 108)*. In Prince Edward Island, the unique structures are the very tall markers such as Annanndale *(see page 106)* and Haszard Point *(see page 100)*.

To mark marine hazards offshore or in channels and estuaries, a great variety of spars and buoys have been used over the years. Noteworthy are the universal red and green buoys and spars to mark the different sides of channels, different shapes to mark different hazards, small towers on buoys with coloured lights or bells, and radar reflectors on floating buoys and low rocks. Coast Guard depots such as the one in Charlottetown are characterized in summer by piles of spars and buoys in for annual repair and painting.

Malpeque Outer Range

The rear light of the Malpeque Outer Range provides an opportunity to see a lighthouse in the middle of a large field given over to agricultural production. It is a classic peppershaker with a broad base and red trim on the door, window, and lamphouse. It is located on private property, but a look back from the road leading to the shore will show the red striped daymark on the seaward side and a glimpse of the front range light between the cottages.

Take Route 20 from Kensingston and follow it beyond the right turn in Malpeque. The lighthouse is visible to the left on the green rise beyond. A little farther on, turn left on the paved Profitt's Point Road and park at the entrance to the private dirt road next to the field.

Darnley Basin and Malpeque Harbour Ranges

In the same general area as the Malpeque Outer Range, several range lights mark the entry to Malpeque Harbour and Darnley Basin. The principal lights are located on the end of Billhook Island, at the west side of the entrance from the sea, and are automated skeleton towers of more or less standard issue.

They are accessible only by boat.

CAPE TRYON

A superb wooden lighthouse sits on Cape Tryon on the north coast of Prince Edward Island, north-northeast of Summerside. Built in 1976 to replace its 1905 predecessor, it is a beautifully crafted square wooden tower supporting a lightly constructed square platform and a square lamphouse with simple rectangular glass panes. Its light flashes for two seconds, then rests for four seconds. Its railings, light windows, and peak are picked out in Coast Guard red. Care must be taken on this site because of the dangerous cliffs, but otherwise it affords a most picturesque lighthouse scene.

This small lighthouse is frequently featured in tourist literature, often pictured with bales of hay or even potatoes in the foreground. It is accessible via a short side road from Route 20. Use the power line as a guide.

New London Range

For the lighthouse enthusiast, the range lights on the northwest side of New London Bay, on the north side of Prince Edward Island, are especially attractive. The modern front range light (right) is an undistinguished square steel tower set on wooden piles in the reddish sand beach. A bright red diamond daymark contrasts its rectangular white lattice front. The real attraction, however, is the back range light (above) with its tapering square tower and small, attached red-roofed house. The tower tapers into a straight-sided square that continues to its lightly built platform and unadorned top. Its hexagonal lanternhouse has simple square glass panes. It is now a cottage and has been decorated with lots of Coast Guard red.

In its grassy setting among the red beaches and dunes, the simple tower with its attached house makes a charming picture. It is accessible by taking a short side road from the coastal Route 6. With the nearby Cape Tryon light, this is a lighthouse destination of note with fine beaches thrown in for good measure.

North Rustico Harbour

A well-maintained 11-metre (36-foot) white tower with a residence attached marks the west side of the entrance to North Rustico Harbour, on the north shore of Prince Edward Island. This lighthouse has seen half a dozen renovations and improvements since a light was first lit in 1876. As with so many Atlantic lights now, every available bit of trim around windows and doors is picked out in Coast Guard red, although the platform itself remains white. Its omnidirectional lens is clearly visible in the red hexagonal lamphouse. An emergency light is attached to one corner of the platform.

This picturesque spot is accessible on a short side road from Route 6, northwest of Charlottetown. In summer, it is a beehive of activity ranging from the serious business of fishing to tourist boat excursions, kayak trips, and camping.

COVEHEAD HARBOUR

The craftsman who built the 8-metre (26-foot) lighthouse tower at Covehead Harbour added distinctive brackets to the underside of its platform, thus ensuring that it would stand out from the crowd of small wooden lighthouses so characteristic of Prince Edward Island. Its feet are firmly planted in the sand dunes at Cape Stanhope, at the west end of Stanhope Beach in Prince Edward Island National Park. The lighthouse marks the entrance to Covehead Harbour, directly north of Charlottetown. Its lanternhouse is a stolid square-windowed structure blinded on the landward side and seasonal in operation. The photograph here is of the Covehead light when it was painted in more traditional lighthouse colours. Now it is decorated to an extreme with gaudy red trim and used as an intrepretive centre in the park.

Head north from Charlottetown on Route 2 and take Route 6 north and west to Stanhope, then turn onto Route 25 into the national park.

As you are leaving Prince Edward Island, you will be reminded of its lighthouse heritage. From the ferry terminal at Wood Islands, the several lighthouses on the point and the pier will catch your attention. On the other Nova Scotia side of the ferry route, the Caribou Island lighthouse stands out. If you return to the mainland via the Confederation Bridge, the lights at Borden and the old ferry terminal will be in view, as will the Cape Jourimain lighthouse on the New Brunswick side.

Cape North lighthouse, Nova Scotia, before its move to Ottawa, with its wooden replacement under construction nearby.

Lighthouses
of
Nova Scotia

Nova Scotia is a province of many coastlines, each distinctive and posing different problems for the navigator and the lighthouse builder. Cape Breton's bold cliffs give way eastward to the shallow, sandy-bottomed Northumberland Strait shoreline all the way to the New Brunswick border. The southeast shore from Yarmouth to Cape Breton is incredibly irregular with bays and inlets, thousands of islands and reefs, and, at Halifax, one of the great natural harbours in the world. This saw-tooth shoreline is open to the full fury of gales sweeping in from the open Atlantic with 15-metre (49-foot) waves not uncommon during the storm season. The Gulf Stream, a huge current of warm ocean water sweeping north up the east side of North America, encounters the icy waters of the south-flowing Labrador Current off Newfoundland and Nova Scotia. The common result is an obscuring fog, sometimes lasting for many weeks.

$\mathcal{D}$ark basaltic cliffs extend from Brier Island, at the entry to the Bay of Fundy, northeast 250 kilometres (155 miles) to Cape Split. They are rarely relieved by inlets or harbours other than Digby Gut. Once inside Minas Basin, extensive red mudflats are exposed each day at low tide, then flooded by the highest tides in the world. Yet from here, millions of tons of gypsum are shipped every year from Avonport in vessels that must come and go on the tide.

For more than 100 years after Champlain wintered at Annapolis in 1605, no lighthouses graced Nova Scotian coasts. Growing merchant and military demands encouraged the contruction of the first lighthouse in Canada at Louisbourg in 1734, followed by the lighthouse on Sambro Island, at the mouth of Halifax Harbour, in 1760. Farther down the shore, lights were built at Cape Roseway and Shelburne in 1788 and 1789, and in the following 20 years, another dozen lights were added. By this time, lighthouses to serve local traffic also were being constructed in many small harbours. These were mostly simple wooden structures of limited range with oil lamps that burned local fuels, such as seal or fish oil. By the mid-19th century, major lights had been established at such vital locations as Cape Forchu, Brier Island, and Seal Island.

With excellent fishing nearby, tiny villages sprang up in dozens of sheltered coves along the eastern coast of Nova Scotia. Some of them blossomed into major fishing centres, such as Yarmouth, Shelburne, and Lunenburg, the latter now a World Heritage Site. As this pattern of settlement developed along with coastal trade and growing naval activity, so did the construction of aids to navigation. The 1998 Canadian Coast Guard List of Lights indicates that Nova Scotia has several hundred navigational aids in the form of lighthouses, range lights, buoys, and channel markers. All lighthouses are now automated and on mainland or solar power.

Of special pride to Nova Scotians was the invention in 1846 by Dr. Abraham Gesner, a physician from Cornwallis, of a technique for distilling kerosene from coal. His new fuel for lamps was first tested at the Maugher's Beach lighthouse, at the mouth of Halifax Harbour, in 1851. It was immediately successful and was quickly adopted in most Canadian and many foreign lightstations. It remained the choice for oil lamps for decades and even persisted in a few Canadian lights into the 1950s.

Now, with universal automation, traditional lighthouse keepers have disappeared from the coasts of Nova Scotia. Their places have been taken by crews of visiting technicians, helicopter pilots, and specialist engineers. Restoration of many of the lightstations is now being carried out by local associations and societies devoted to preserving maritime history.

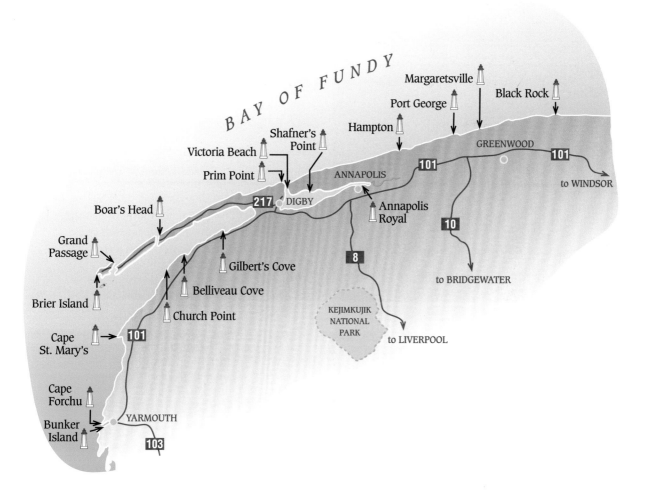

*T*his is part of the
*Evangeline Trail of tourist literature that runs from
the southwest tip of Nova Scotia at Yarmouth along the south shore of the
Bay of Fundy. Its lights showed the way into Bay of Fundy ports and
small fishing communities in an area marked by
very high tides.*

CAPE FORCHU ◄

Travelers on the ferries between Nova Scotia and Maine pass in front of Cape Forchu on the outer reaches of Yarmouth Harbour, a site whose history goes back to early Portuguese explorers. The lighthouse here serves local shipping but also points the way into the Bay of Fundy.

A fine octagonal wooden tower was built on the point in 1839. Later, a tall round Chance Brothers lamphouse and a second-order Fresnel lens were installed. In 1962, the old tower was replaced with a slender reinforced concrete tower 21 metres (69 feet) high. The daymark of the airport-style beacon has the same red and white vertical stripes as the old wooden tower. The lighthouse is now equipped with dual electronic horns that blow in unison at 130 and 190 degrees. The light is now much reduced in power, but it still flashes, and the horn is still useful to local fishermen in the frequent fogs. The original Fresnel lens from Cape Forchu is on display at the county museum in Yarmouth.

From central Yarmouth, take Main Street north, turn left onto Vancouver Street, and left again onto Route 304. From there, signs indicate the route to the lightstation. The neat grounds and gardens, the informative signs, and the walkways up to the museum in the former keeper's house are maintained by the Friends of the Yarmouth Museum and are a credit to them.

BUNKER ISLAND ►

On the way to Cape Forchu, a lighthouse is visible on Bunker Island at the end of a spit across the harbour. It is best viewed from a pullout and parking area beside a monument to Yarmouth seamen, partway down the Cape Forchu road. It can also be viewed from the fishing wharves at the causeway near Forchu. This is a square concrete tower rising from a square service building, the whole set on a caisson-like structure at the end of a bouldery spit. Its red lamphouse has outward-sloping rectangular windows similar to the type used in airport control towers. Its daymark is a bold red vertical stripe.

Access is possible but difficult at low tide from the Sand Beach Road off the shore road on the east side of Yarmouth Harbour.

CAPE ST. MARY'S

The modern square concrete tower at Cape St. Mary's, on the corner of a square service building, houses an automated light. On this site, a traditional white wooden tower was built in 1868. Hiking trails lead along the cliffed shore near the lightstation.

Turn off coastal Route 1 onto the Cape St. Mary's Road near Mavillette. Continue for about 3 kilometres (2 miles) to almost the end of the road among fishing sheds, then turn right onto a small gravel side road that leads over a hill to the lighthouse.

CHURCH POINT ▲

A peppershaker lighthouse sits near the shore over-looking St. Mary's Bay at Church Point on Lighthouse Road off coastal Route 1. Tidal waters surge in and out of the bay, and the islands of Digby Neck are visible across the water. St. Anne's College, in Church Point, maintains the lighthouse and the nearby walking trails.

BELLIVEAU COVE ◀

A small lighthouse sits at the end of the dock at Belliveau Cove on the old coastal road, Route 1. This nicely maintained peppershaker lighthouse of recent origin is unusual in its tall lanternhouse and ornate wooden railing. High tide in St. Mary's Bay fills the harbour slip at the lighthouse, but low tide leaves it high and dry with extensive mudflats between the docks and water.

Turn off Route 101 at Exit 28, drive south to the old Route 1, and turn left at the intersection. The lighthouse is readily visible from the road.

GILBERT'S COVE ▶

St. Mary's Bay, between the mainland and Digby Neck and its extension in Long and Brier islands, was an important shipping centre for Digby County lumber and for wooden ship construction. In 1904, a lighthouse was erected on a small projection into the bay at Gilbert's Point. It is now a Nova Scotia heritage property, with a museum and tearoom, situated in a small park. The white keeper's house with its wooden lanternhouse at the centre looks about the same as it did when first built. By 1960, the lighthouse had been shuttered up and provided with an automatic beacon. By 1970, with the continuing decline in lumbering, fishing, and coastal trade, it was slated for demolition but luckily it was rescued by the Gilbert's Cove and District Historical Society.

The Gilbert's Cove lighthouse is readily visible from the main highway, Route 1. Take the short connecting lane to the parking area at the lighthouse. In summer, it is open to visitors and provides displays of local history. On the ground floor, the historical society operates a small tearoom and a gift shop selling local crafts.

PRIM POINT (DIGBY GUT) ◀

Digby Gut has long been the entry point into the Annapolis Basin, a protected bay on an otherwise exposed coast. Micmacs were known to have come here by canoe across the Bay of Fundy from the mouth of the Saint John River, 69 kilometres (43 miles) away. In 1605, Samuel de Champlain came in through the narrow "gut" and journeyed up the basin to found one of the earliest settlements in North America at Annapolis Royal. By 1817, commerce and settlement justified building a lighthouse on the west side of the entrance at Prim Point.

The usual square wooden tower, with oil lamps and reflectors, sat on top of the keeper's house. Its replacement in the 1870s apparently began the tradition of the daymark being a broad red vertical stripe. The modern light, automated and unmanned, is a square concrete tower on the northeast corner of a square service building with the typical red stripe on each seaward face.

This is the lighthouse that passengers on the Saint John–Digby ferry see on their way to the Digby terminal. It is readily accessible via a side road off the main road running between the ferry terminal and the town of Digby.

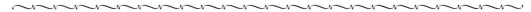

Boar's Head and Grand Passage

A long slender peninsula of dark basaltic rock extends southwest from Digby. With its extension in Long and Brier islands, it forms the northwest boundary of St. Mary's Bay. Narrow channels mark geological faults that cut through the spine of the peninsula in two places at Tiverton and Westport, forming harbours for fishermen. Each is marked with a lighthouse, buoys, and range markers.

The first channel gap is between East Ferry and Tiverton (above), where settlement was first established in 1785. The Boar's Head light, built in 1864, is located at the northern end of Long Island. To reach the lighthouse, turn right immediately after disembarking from the ferry at Tiverton and follow the road over the hill. There you will find a standard tapering four-square tower with a red lamphouse. It has a splendid view of the bay and passage.

The lighthouse at Westport, on the northern end of Brier Island across the second gut, is known as the Grand Passage light and is a standard square tower on the corner of a concrete service building. Its lamphouse is of the modern control-tower type with sloping rectangular panes. To reach the lighthouse, follow Westport's main street, Water Street, to its end.

BRIER ISLAND ▶

Apart from the scenery, the real attraction on Route 217 along Digby Neck and the islands is the lighthouse at the southern tip of Brier Island. Its origins are linked to the flood of Loyalists who came north from New England into the Bay of Fundy, where in 1783 they founded the city of Saint John. As sea traffic increased to this and other centres, so did the need for lighthouses. One of the earliest was a substantial lighthouse completed on the southern tip of Brier Island in 1809. The original wooden tower was replaced in 1944 by the present octagonal reinforced concrete tower with its flaring concrete platform and aluminum lamphouse. The power source for the light is now mainline electricity. Its arresting daymark consists of three red bands on the red-capped white tower.

The Brier Island lighthouse is located in a spectacular location with the sea breaking all around onto black basaltic rocks. It sits astride the great flushing tides of Fundy, which bring up rich nutrient-laden waters that attract schools of small fish, seabirds, dolphins, and whales.

ANNAPOLIS ROYAL ◀

The old lighthouse at Annapolis Royal sits in the midst of gardens, lawns, and boardwalks along the town waterfront. Built in 1889, it is still operational, but more as a tourist information centre than a marine light. It is a peppershaker with fancy railings around its platform and a square lamphouse that shows a red light on two sides. This lighthouse is situated in the middle of an historic area, with Fort Anne and Port Royal nearby. Port Royal, founded in 1605, is home to many historic buildings.

Access to the Annapolis Royal lighthouse is via Exit 22 from Route 101.

SCHAFNER'S POINT ▲

A drive of about 11 kilometres (7 miles) beyond Annapolis Royal brings you to Port Royal, first occupied in 1605 and one of the earliest European settlements in North America. Now it is restored as the Habitation, a national historic site. Schafner's Point is located about 1 kilometre (0.6 miles) beyond that on the seaward side. The lighthouse, constructed in 1885, is a tapering square wooden tower capped with a platform and an old-style hexagonal lamphouse. It sits in a field overlooking the upper end of the Annapolis Basin. Next to it is a small stone monument to lost seafarers.

VICTORIA BEACH ▶

The road to Schafner's Point continues down and around the shore of Digby Gut to a very small lighthouse at Victoria Beach. Almost lost now within houses and fishing establishments, it is visible from the ferry to Saint John.

LIGHTHOUSES OF ATLANTIC CANADA

HAMPTON

The Fundy shore of Nova Scotia is marked by more or less continuous low cliffs from Digby northeast to Cape Split. Here and there, however, small coves and inlets, usually at the mouths of small brooks, provide partial shelter for fishing boats. One of these is at Hampton, opposite Bridgetown, on the main highway, Route 101, through the Annapolis Valley and off Exit 20.

Built in 1911, it sits a little aloof and back from the sea with its neatly painted tapering square tower 9 metres (30 feet) high and capped by a simple square lanternhouse. The seascape is typical of tidal Fundy with boats nodding at their collars at high tide but sitting disconsolately on the exposed sea bottom at low tide a few hours later.

Port George.

Port George

Port George is another of the small coves and harbours on the Fundy shore opposite Middleton on Nova Scotia Route 101, off Exit 18. The local shore road runs northeast alongside this small peppershaker lighthouse with Bay of Fundy's tidal waters within a few metres and boats drawn up alongside. Traditional ship building can still be witnessed occasionally around Port George.

MARGARETSVILLE ▲

A squat square lighthouse has stood on the point beside the Margaretsville breakwater and harbour since 1859. Its daymark is a single broad black horizontal band, and, rare in Canadian lightstations, it has a black roof and black trim around the platform. Local community groups clearly cherish this lighthouse and have constructed walkways and a viewing deck. This spot is known for the legend of a wrecker who lured ships to disaster but who eventually lost his own life in the process.

BLACK ROCK ▶

Canada Creek is a tiny picturesque harbour on the Fundy coast of Nova Scotia, northeast toward Minas Channel and Cape Split. At high tide, these harbours are full and accessible, and at low tide, they are empty with boats resting on the exposed bottom. Nearby and accessible from Canada Creek is a lighthouse on a point called Black Rock, which has displayed a light since 1848. The modern one is a slim round steel tower 9 metres (30 feet) high with two red bands as its daymark and an exposed flashing light on top. In clear weather, the view across Minas Channel, with its tremendous tidal surges twice each day, includes Cape d'Or on the other side and Cape Split away to the northeast.

Lighthouses along this part of the Fundy coast are accessible by local roads that lead across North Mountain from Route 101 in the vicinity of Berwick and Middleton.

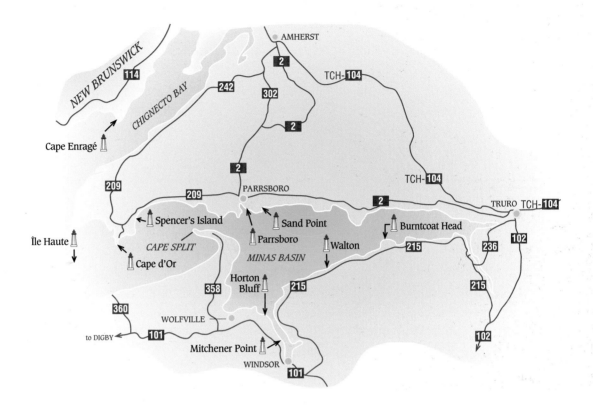

At the head of the
Bay of Fundy, several lighthouses serve local traffic
and the large bulk carriers in the gypsum trade. They share the world's
most extreme tides, as much as 16 metres (53 feet) in the Minas Basin.
All shipping, large and small, must come and go
on the tide.

Horton Bluff

Minas Basin, at the head of the Bay of Fundy, has the highest tides in the world at about 16 metres (53 feet). At high tide, the basin is full and looks like any shoreline, but at low tide, extensive mudflats are exposed with an exceptional array of microlife and feeding birds. The estuary of the Avon River leads off the Minas Basin on the south side. Smaller boats and oceangoing ships, mostly for transportation of gypsum from the Windsor area, enter and leave the estuary at high tide.

At Horton Bluff, northwest of the principal port at Hantsport, a square concrete tower with a red vertical daymark is joined to a square concrete building. It is a back-range light.

The lighthouse is accessed by taking Exit 9 off Nova Scotia Route 101 and following along the shore road.

MITCHENER POINT

At Mitchener Point, a red circular steel tower with two white bands for daymarks supports a flashing light. Mitchener Point is accessed by taking Exit 9 off Nova Scotia Route 101 and following along the shore road.

Walton

Walton is a village on the south shore of Minas Basin, east from Windsor on Route 101 and west from Truro on Route 102. A small wooden lighthouse sits on the cliffs at the mouth of the Walton River to guide ships to dockside. It is open to the public in summer, and visitors can climb to the omnidirectional lamp and view the bay. This is a quiet time in Walton's history, which saw a boom in shipbuilding during the 19th century and another in mining during the mid-20th century. Empty derelict silos and piers mark the dock where 10 million tons of barite was shipped. No longer functional, the lighthouse is now a heritage property of the municipality of East Hants, which has developed a small park around it.

Take the shore road, Route 215, to Walton and turn down the pier road past the dock.

Burntcoat Head ▶

Farther east up the wedge-shaped Minas Basin, at the head of the Bay of Fundy, tidal movements become extreme. In river estuaries, the tide sometimes comes in as a tidal bore, a wall of advancing water. Coastal erosion and deposition are more and more evident up the Minas Basin. At Burntcoat Head, a lighthouse was built on a point of land that, as a result of erosion, soon became an island. In 1913, a larger lighthouse was built on the nearby mainland. It lasted until 1972, when a skeleton tower took over its functions.

A reconstruction of the 1913 lighthouse now stands in Burntcoat Head Park. It represents a type of lighthouse construction common in the late 19th century with its lanternhouse atop a square residence. Other such lighthouses can be seen at Port Bickerton on the Guysborough shore and at Gilbert's Cove south of Digby.

Take the shore road, Route 215, to a shoreward loop that runs between Noel or Minasville. From this point a very small sign indicates the side road to the park and lighthouse. Tidal mudflats in the area provide wonderful viewings of migrating shorebirds in season.

Sand Point and Parrsboro ▶

An example of a movable lighthouse is at Sand Point near Five Islands on Route 2 along the north side of Minas Basin on the way to Parrsboro. This simple little peppershaker lighthouse was constructed in 1913. After erosion gobbled up the first site, it was moved farther back from the sea in 1952. It was moved again in 1957 and again in 1996 to its present location in the Sand Point Campground, where it is cared for by the Five Islands Lighthouse Preservation Society.

The area features wonderful coastal scenery with steep-sided islands, tidal flats, and numerous shorebirds. It is also widely known for its mineral collecting, with zeolites and agates of special note.

Parrsboro, the largest town on the north side of the Minas Basin, was once a principal shipping port and a ferry terminal for crossing to Kingsport. A lighthouse was built at the end of the sandbar on the east side of the harbour, which at high tide was navigable by medium-sized vessels. The modern light is a standard white square concrete tower on the corner of a square service building.

It is accessible on foot from the end of Wharf Road, south of Parrsboro town centre. The lighthouse is also visible in the middle distance from the road along the west side of the harbour on the way to Partridge Island.

Parrsboro, the old port and business centre, is now a tourist destination with a worldwide reputation for fossils—dinosaurs, primitive plants, and footprints—as well as its mineral specimens. The local museum displays these assets well.

SPENCER'S ISLAND

A short loop off the coastal highway, Route 209, takes visitors to the beach at Spencer's Island and a white lighthouse at water's edge, now a municipal heritage building. Pilings just below the lighthouse indicate where a wharf existed in busier times. This is a lovely spot to pause and take in the scenery, with the tidal action in the Minas Channel just offshore, seabirds all about, distant views of the other side of the bay and a feeling of history.

One of the great mysteries of the sea began here when the vessel *Marie Celeste* was launched from the shore nearby. In 1872, she was discovered abandoned at sea with sails aloft, dinner places set, everything normally in place, and not a soul aboard. No one has ever discovered the fate of the *Marie Celeste*'s crew.

Cape d'Or ▲

Cape d'Or lightstation sits on the north side of Minas Channel at the head of the Bay of Fundy, on a point of dark volcanic rock dating from the Triassic Age when dinosaurs ruled the planet. At high tide, the site is nearly surrounded by water, but six hours later, at low tide, it is high and dry with expanses of dark rocks, kelp, and bouldery beaches below the cliffs. The original light, built in 1922, was later replaced with the present square concrete tower on the corner of a square service building. It is a modest station and long since automated, but it boasts a summer tearoom and guesthouse in the old keeper's quarters set amidst some spectacular Atlantic scenery.

The Cape d'Or lightstation still guides ships in and out of Minas Basin. These include local boats and oceangoing freighters carrying as much as two million tons of rock gypsum a year from the Windsor area to ports along the eastern seaboard of the United States. Captains carefully plan their voyages around the movement of the tides.

This lighthouse is accessible from the coastal highway, Route 209, west of Parrsboro and just west of Cape Spencer near East Advocate. Signs for Cape d'Or lead for a short distance along a paved side road and then onto a gravel road that continues for some 5.5 kilometres (3.5 miles) to a parking lot above the cape. A short but steep walking road leads to the lightstation and a tremendous view.

Île Haute

Île Haute appears as a dark steep-sided island well out in the Bay of Fundy, off the peninsula that includes Cape d'Or and Cape Chignecto. On fine days, visitors can see it from several points along the Fundy coast, such as at Cape d'Or, at the shoreline between Margaretsville and Black Rock, and at Quaco, New Brunswick. For many years, a lightstation sat on the island's high point, but now a skeleton tower with an automatic light is all that remains. When I visited in about 1990, it was unoccupied. Île Haute is located in the midst of fierce tidal currents as the waters of the Bay of Fundy surge in and out to make the highest tides in the world a few nautical miles to the northeast in Minas Basin. Île Haute is inaccessible except by helicopter or boat when weather and tides permit.

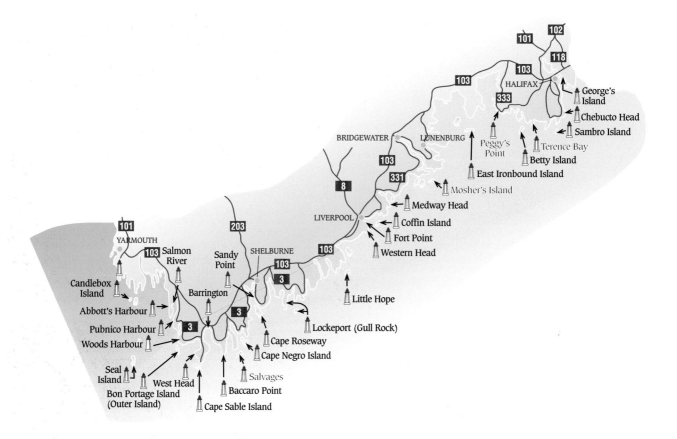

102
101
118
103
103
HALIFAX
George's Island
333
Chebucto Head
BRIDGEWATER
LUNENBURG
Peggy's Point
Sambro Island
Terence Bay
103
Betty Island
East Ironbound Island
8
331
Mosher's Island
Medway Head
LIVERPOOL
Coffin Island
101
203
SHELBURNE
103
Fort Point
YARMOUTH
103
Salmon River
Sandy Point
103
Western Head
Candlebox Island
Barrington
3
Abbott's Harbour
Little Hope
3
Pubnico Harbour
3
Lockeport (Gull Rock)
Woods Harbour
Cape Roseway
Seal Island
Cape Negro Island
West Head
Salvages
Bon Portage Island (Outer Island)
Baccaro Point
Cape Sable Island

*T*his part of the
Lighthouse Route of tourist literature runs along
the south shore from Yarmouth at the southwest tip of Nova Scotia
to Halifax. It is rich in lighthouses of great variety, from the massive wooden
tower on Seal Island to the concrete tower at Western Head to the skeleton steel range
light at Eddy Point. Many of them, such as Peggy's Point, are readily
accessible, while others are on remote offshore islands.
The shore is well served by trunk highways
and local roads.

Candlebox Island ▶

One of the offshore islands near Yarmouth once had a feature that a Coast Guard helicopter pilot went out of his way to show me with delight. As we neared the tiny and treeless Candlebox Island, with its house on one side and a small undistinguished lighthouse on the other, he pointed out a well-worn path in the peaty soil that encircled the property. He claimed that once every day for many years, the lighthouse keeper took his exercise by running determinedly round and round his tiny empire. As we circled in the helicopter and looked down, I could only think of Alexander Selkirk: "I am monarch of all I survey . . . from centre all round to the sea" (William Cowper, "The Solitude of Alexander Selkirk," *Palgreave's Golden Treasury*, 1875).

Access is only by helicopter or boat.

Salmon River ▶

Here and there along the Lighthouse Route are displaced lighthouses that were moved from their original sites for commercial purposes or for preservation. One of these is now at Middle West Pubnico, moved about 80 kilometres (50 miles) to the southeast in 1980 at the end of its useful life at Salmon River, north of Yarmouth. Now it is a nicely maintained part of an Acadian craft shop.

Take Exit 31 off Route 103, or leave coastal Route 3 at Pubnico, and take Route 335 for about 2 kilometres (1.25 miles) to the lighthouse.

ABBOTT'S HARBOUR ▶

A standard wooden peppershaker at Abbott's Harbour is situated in a lovely park setting in an area surrounded by fishing villages, boats, and numerous offshore islands.

Access is from Route 335, 3.5 kilometres (2 miles) past the Salmon River lighthouse. Turn right onto the paved road marked Abbott's Harbour and continue for 1.6 kilometres (1 mile) to reach Lighthouse Park.

PUBNICO HARBOUR ◀

On Pubnico Harbour's Beach Point is a small lighthouse of unusual design. A slightly tapering metal tower leads to a narrow platform and an octagonal lamphouse with flat panes sloping outward to a nearly flat roof. Its daymark is unique in that the tower is white on the bottom half and red above. A small service building with a foghorn stands nearby.

Erosion is natural on any point or sandbar, and the first lighthouse and residence on the point, built in 1854, became isolated when erosion cut it off from the mainland. It was rebuilt in 1908 in a new location.

The modern lighthouse is protected by a breakwater on the seaward side. This is a lovely spot on a fine day with the island-studded shoreline and the sea all around.

Near Charlesville on the coastal road, Route 3, take the gravel road marked Lighthouse Road and drive about 1/3 kilometre (0.2 miles). A short walk takes you along the sandbar to the lighthouse.

WOODS HARBOUR ▶

The coastal road in the southwest corner of Nova Scotia, Route 3, passes through several settlements on the east side of Woods Harbour between Charlesville and Shag Harbour. Clearly visible from the main road, a lighthouse sits on a small low island opposite a cluster of wharves and fishing boats. A square white tower with a red lanternhouse, the Woods Harbour light stands about 7 metres (23 feet) high, including the base pier, and sits directly on the gravel bar (Big Ledge) at tide level. It is a coastal marker for local traffic in a waterway studded with islands and reefs.

Bon Portage Island (or Outer Island)

In 1874, a modest four-sided lighthouse tower, with residence attached, was built on the south end of Bon Portage Island, off the south end of the Nova Scotia coast. For its first 55 years, the changing seasons were the principal events, with keepers coming and going and an occasional shipwreck nearby. In 1898, for example, the steamship *Express* went ashore just below the light. It has since slowly disintegrated, leaving bits of rusted steel among the shore boulders. Then, in 1926, Morrill Richardson and his new bride, Evelyn, bought the 285-hectare (704-acre) island for a small mixed farming operation in the hope that one day they could become keepers of the Bon Portage Island light. In the spring of 1929, the job was theirs, and a new chapter for the light began.

For the next 15 years, the Richardsons worked hard at fixing up the site and repairing the leaky, drafty lighthouse. They cleared and improved the land, and raised their family in a world of oil lamps and woodstoves, with no running water and only outdoor plumbing. Communication with the outside world required a trip in a small boat across open ocean. In emergencies, they raised a flag on the lighthouse to alert friends on the mainland to their distress. Yet for all this, they had a good family life, enough wordly goods to get by, and an inspiring closeness to nature. Evelyn wrote about their life in a wonderfully sensitive book, *We Keep a Light*. It became a best-seller and won the Governor General's Award for 1945. It has recently been reprinted.

The old tower and house are long gone, replaced by a square concrete tower with an electric light and modern keepers' houses. Now, beside the automated lightstation, the Richardsons' hard-won fields, the pathways along the shore beside the saltwater ponds and the swamps, and the windblown woods where they loved to walk are a bird sanctuary that is part of a research station. Even the name has reverted to the post-Acadian, pre-Loyalist Outer Island in modern listings.

Bon Portage Island lightstation is accessible by boat from Shag Harbour, located on the coastal road, Route 3. The lighthouse is visible from some spots on the road, notably from the grounds of the Evelyn Richardson Memorial School.

SEAL ISLAND

In about 1820, two families, the Crowells and the Hickens, settled on this island off the southernmost tip of Nova Scotia to do a little farming and to aid distressed mariners cast ashore. As shipwrecks increased in number, petitions resulted in the construction in 1830 of a splendid lighthouse. The Crowells and the Hickens were the first keepers.

The tapering octagonal tower about 21 metres (69 feet) high remains a fine example of frame construction of the period. Inside, four flights of wooden stairs lead from the ground floor to the lamphouse past the original hand-hewn timbers. The timbers are held together by treenails, hardwood pegs driven through matching holes bored by hand. The use of supporting "knees," massive right-angled pieces cut from the spreading roots of tamarack trees, and the treenail method of fastening were common in the heyday of wooden shipbuilding in the Maritimes during the 19th century.

The tower is shingled and painted white with a daymark of two broad red horizontal bands. When I first visited Seal Island in 1979, the original Chance Brothers round cast-iron lanternhouse and its second-order Fresnel lens were still in service. These were replaced in 1980 with a new aluminum lamphouse with eight flat sides and an airport-style beacon light. The beautiful original glass lens is now located in a replica of the lamphouse administered by the local museum in Barrington.

Now, with automation, summer seas sparkle only for passing fishermen, and winter storms toss huge waves against the lonely shoreline without witness. Solar panels and banks of batteries power the light held aloft in the old timbered tower, alone in the night and fog, still ready to guide mariners in and out of the Bay of Fundy.

The original lighthouse, with its wonderful workmanship, still exists on Seal Island. Access is only by water or air.

The hand-hewn "knees" at Seal Island lighthouse.

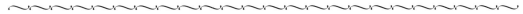

West Head ◄

When you leave coastal Route 3 and drive down Route 330 toward Cape Sable Island, over the causeway and along the shore, you pass numerous fishing establishments. At one of these, West Head, a stolid little steel tower, plain and round, stands on a point beside the large fish plant. At the first *WELCOME TO CLARK'S HARBOUR* sign, a short side road leads to the lighthouse. The present light is mundane, but it marks a spot where a light has stood since 1888.

Clark's Harbour is where the famous Cape Islander originated, a type of fishing boat with high flaring bows to breast big seas and a long flat open working area aft of the wheelhouse. Cape Islanders are a common sight along the coasts of eastern Canada and even the United States, piled high with lobster pots on the way out to sea. They are safe, fast, and graceful on the sea.

Cape Sable Island ▼

Long sand and gravel spits sweep south from Clark's Harbour to form the southernmost point of Nova Scotia. These were a constant hazard to navigation. After the *Hungarian* was lost with all hands off Cape Sable in a winter storm in early 1860, the Nova Scotia government built a lightstation on the point.

The lighthouse there now is a slender white tapering concrete tower about 27 metres (89 feet) high. The automated electric lamp and lens system in the red octagonal lamphouse sends out a beam that is usually visible for 24 kilometres (15 miles) in clear weather, much less in the notorious fogs that frequent the area.

The station was destaffed in 1986 and the outbuildings burned in 1988, leaving this beautiful tower to stand alone. It is accessible only by boat but is visible as a slender needle on the horizon from the beach below Clark's Harbour. The viewpoint is accessed by turning off the coastal road, Route 3, and following the signs on Route 330 to Clark's Harbour. From there, at the sign for The Hawk, turn left and follow the road to the end.

Barrington ◀

This book includes few nonfunctioning lighthouses (ones that have been moved and now serve as restaurants, bars, or souvenir shops) or skeleton towers, unless they are of particular note. At Barrington, however, a replica of the top of the Seal Island lighthouse is noteworthy. It was constructed by a local group, and the magnificent original lanternhouse and lens were installed. It is now run as the Seal Island Light Museum. This is one of the few places where visitors can see one of the beautiful old lanternhouses of the mid-19th century close up. *(See listing for Seal Island, page 152, for a photograph of the lanternhouse on its original tower.)*

Baccaro Point ▶

Baccaro Point on the east side of the entrance to Barrington Bay in Shelburne County is the southernmost point on the Nova Scotia mainland and, surprisingly, a few minutes of latitude farther south than Toronto and at the same latitude as northernmost California. Lighthouses on Seal Island and on Cape Sable Island, not far to the east, are a few minutes of latitude even farther south than the Baccaro lighthouse.

A lighthouse was built on Baccaro Point in 1850, long before roads reached the point. Construction materials had to be hauled along the beaches because boats could not land on the bouldery granite point. The original lighthouse was replaced by the present structure in 1976. It is a square tower about 14 metres (46 feet) high with an octagonal lanternhouse on a square platform with a light railing. Inside, an omnidirectional lens with a winking electric bulb gives its characteristic three flashes every ten seconds. Its electronic foghorn, on a separate stand near the tower, points south out to sea with a two-second blast every 20 seconds.

When I visited in 1980, the lighthouse was almost lost within a complex defense establishment with radar domes and support buildings. When I visited in 1998, the lighthouse stood alone with parts of foundations of the keepers' house and service buildings nearby. On that visit, the lighthouse point was right at the edge of a drifting fogbank. Especially dramatic was the sound of heavy engines as a large fishing boat passed the point, invisible in the dense fog but close by and presumably within hearing distance of Baccaro's warning signals.

Local hydro lines supply the automated station. A local road leads to it from Port La Tour, just off the old coastal Route 109, ending at a parking and picnic area. A sign warns not to stand too close to the foghorn, a few metres from the tower, because it comes on without warning whenever the radar sensors detect fog offshore.

Salvages ◀

A square house with a lighthouse tower protruding from the centre of its roof perches on the low wave-washed rocks of a shoal area called The Salvages, just east of Baccaro and visible from there. Long since automated with an array of electronic horns and solar panels, it serves the heavy traffic of fishing boats and coastal vessels. On my visit to nearby Baccaro in 1998, its horn was clearly audible in the thick fogbank that usually blankets the area on warm summer days. Access is only by helicopter or boat.

CAPE NEGRO ISLAND

Cape Negro is another in a series of lighthouses in close proximity to one another along the southeast coast of Nova Scotia between Yarmouth and Halifax. Its standard hexagonal concrete tower with a red lamphouse now stands alone on a low flat coastal island, a little back from the shore about halfway between Baccaro and Cape Roseway. It is accessible only by boat.

Cape Roseway

The third lighthouse built in Nova Scotia, Cape Roseway on McNutt's Island outside Shelburne, was constructed of stone quarried on site in 1788. According to local lore, even the mortar was made on the island by burning mussel shells. Its first lamp burned seal oil. The first foghorn, installed in 1831, was a cannon, as was the custom of the day.

The old light was replaced in 1977 by an octagonal concrete tower with a white platform and red railings. Its octagonal lamphouse some 17 metres (56 feet) high on a base about 15 metres (49 feet) above sea level is visible for some 26 kilometres (16 miles). Its deep-voiced diaphone boomed out over the sea until 1972, when electronic horns were installed. In 1998, sad-looking service buildings and keepers' houses lay abandoned and boarded up, awaiting demolition or removal.

This station is accessible from Gunning Cove by boat with a 3-kilometre (2-mile) walk across the island.

SANDY POINT

An unusual lighthouse stands on a square concrete block at the end of a spit that is exposed at low tide on the east side of outer Shelburne Harbour. Shelburne is an old Nova Scotia community, and a light has been at this site since 1873. The present square wooden tower, built in 1976, supports a fixed red range light in a red lanternhouse. A small park and swimming beach, with a parking lot, make an attractive spot for a picnic. At low tide, visitors can walk to the base of the lighthouse.

Take Exit 25 from Route 103 into Shelburne. At the main downtown intersection, follow the signs for Sandy Point to the lighthouse and the park, about 8 kilometres (5 miles) down the east side of Shelburne Harbour.

LOCKEPORT

A rectangular concrete dwelling with a red-capped square concrete tower emerging from its roof occupies a barren wind-swept granite island in the centre of the entry channel to Lockeport Harbour about 5 kilometres (3 miles) south of Lockeport village. Two auxiliary buildings had disappeared by 1998, leaving only debris-cluttered foundations.

The lighthouse was built in 1853 and had a variety of oil lamps and lenses. Now it is an electric bulb in an omnidirectional lens with a computer-controlled flash sequence. An array of solar cells supplies power for the light and electronic horns.

This lightstation is accessible only by air or by boat in rare calm weather. It is, however, visible from Lockeport village at the corner of South Street and the beach, and also from the end of the road at Western Head. *(See listing for Western Head, page 159).*

Another lighthouse is visible from the dock area in Lockeport Harbour. A slender round red-topped tower (above) with a red band about two-thirds of the way up stands beside a small service building on Carter's Island just off the harbour mouth.

Gull Rock.

Solar panels and electronic horns on Gull Rock.

Little Hope ▲

Little Hope Island, a patch of boulders little more than a couple of metres above sea level, has room for seabirds to spread their drying wings but little else. About 16 kilometres (10 miles) from Liverpool and 3 kilometres (2 miles) offshore, its 23.5-metre (77-foot) concrete tower with modest buttresses supports a small light powered by solar panels. Beside its base, the foundation of the old keeper's house is often occupied by a flock of cormorants, locally called shags, sunning themselves.

On fine days, visitors can see the light offshore from the road to St. Catherine's River down the west side of the seaside adjunct of Kejimkujik National Park, south of Port Mouton and Port Joli on Route 103.

Western Head ▶

A standard octagonal concrete tower built in 1962 stands at the entrance to Liverpool Harbour. The site—formerly a compound including a light tower, residence, service buildings, and radio tower—was automated in 1988. It now sits conspicuously alone on its bare point with a tiny service building, the tall radio tower, and a bank of electronic foghorns. A concrete retaining wall protects the area along the edge of the wave-washed bouldery shoreline. Like many of the lightstations along this coast, it is completely exposed to the open Atlantic. Be wary of large rogue waves, and don't wander too far out on the shore.

The Western Head lighthouse is readily accessible from Breakwater Road, a loop south-east from Main Street in Liverpool. Stop along the way to visit Fort Point Lighthouse Park in Liverpool. *(See listing for Fort Point, page 160).*

Fort Point ▲

The third oldest surviving lighthouse in Nova Scotia sits in Fort Point Lighthouse Park, a delightful stopping point at the end of Main Street in Liverpool. The demands of a booming lumber trade, with the consequent increase in shipping, led to its construction in 1855. The building, an odd assortment of angles and peaks, has a small square lanternhouse with plain glass windows at the front.

From the time it was built until it was closed in 1989, the old light was a landmark in Liverpool Harbour. From 1920–1950, the building also provided weather forecasts for local shipping by hoisting various signals in the form of large wicker balls, baskets, and cones. Its reflectors behind the lamps were polished so often that the silvering was worn down to the copper and it is said that in its final days its light was a warm coppery hue. The lens is still visible in the lamproom.

In the peaceful setting existing now, it is difficult to realize that this point of land witnessed the departure and arrival of privateers who stalked American shipping during the American Revolution and again in the War of 1812. Vignettes from this chapter of Canadian history are depicted inside the small museum and on the grounds. Staff in period costume, some local lighthouse history and a climb to the lamproom with a view are also featured.

This gem of an old lighthouse and park, with its outstanding rose garden, is easily reached by following Main Street in Liverpool to its end.

Coffin Island ▶

A solitary white hexagonal concrete tower 16 metres (53 feet) high stands on the south end of Coffin Island off the mouth of Liverpool Bay, on the south shore of Nova Scotia. A boulder-filled cribwork protects the easily eroded shore in front of the light.

The structure was built in 1914 following a lightning strike on the old station and a destructive fire. The station was automated in 1962. Only the tower now survives, but foundations of earlier service buildings can still be seen in the adjacent rocky clearing. Erosion is once again threatening the light, and residents from nearby communities are rallying to save it.

Coffin Island lighthouse is visible from the shore road south of Liverpool. Access is by boat.

Medway Head

A square white tapering tower 8.5 metres (28 feet) tall sits on the point at the west side of the entry to Medway Harbour. A simple square lanternhouse with flat glass panes caps its wide flaring platform. The first lighthouse constructed here in 1851 was replaced with the present tower in 1983. On a rise near the lighthouse, a red-peaked roof, shutters, and widow's walk mark a surprisingly large private residence for such an isolated place. It is said to be the relocated residence of the former keeper. The sea view from this lightstation is superb.

Medway Head is accessible at the end of Long Cove Road, out of Port Medway via Exit 17A on Route 103, 30 kilometres (19 miles) south of Bridgewater.

Mosher's Island ▶

A white circular tower stands on Mosher's Island at the west side of the entrance to the La Have River, just south of Lunenburg. The original square pyramidal wooden tower, built in 1868, lasted more than a century. This photograph was taken in 1989 when a replacement tower had been installed, but the original tower had yet to be demolished. Regrettably, in 1999, little was left but the automated new tower.

The lighthouse is accessible only by boat from Dublin Shore or nearby.

East Ironbound Island ▲

Rising like an church steeple from the front of a small oblong two-storey dwelling, this 12-metre (39-foot) square tower is part of the string of coastal lights south and west of Halifax Harbour. A unique charm comes from its white shingle siding, bright red roof, and platform with red railings and a polygonal lamphouse and festoons of supporting cables. This lighthouse was built in 1867 and has long been automated.

East Ironbound Island is only accessible by sea or helicopter.

Peggy's Point (commonly known as Peggy's Cove)

A lighthouse was built on Peggy's Point at the east side of the entrance to St. Margaret's Bay in 1868. In 1979, it was replaced by the present tapering white octagonal concrete tower, which is 15 metres (49 feet) high. Its base sits on the point's bare massive granite rock, and the sides flare at the top to form the platform. Its lamphouse is of plain aluminum with flat glass panes.

The lighthouse, with its automated light, is unique for having a post office in its base, where letters and postcards can be sent on their way with a special cancellation. In September 1998, it witnessed a flood of the world's press, the Royal Canadian Mounted Police, the Canadian Coast Guard, local rescue craft, and onlookers in the aftermath of the tragic crash of Swissair Flight 111 only a few kilometres offshore. Memorials to the victims have been erected near the lighthouse.

The location is officially Peggy's Point but is known to millions as the Peggy's Cove lighthouse, after the picturesque fishing village close by. It is readily accessible on Route 333, 40 kilometres (25 miles) from Halifax. In summer, the area teems with tourists from all over the world.

BETTY ISLAND

Halfway between two of Canada's most famous lighthouses at Sambro and at Peggy's Point visitors will find the Betty Island lighthouse. Built in 1875, it was a square two-storey structure with a light tower on a platform at the peak of its roof. In 1986, this was replaced by a four-sided wooden pyramid with a red lamphouse and a fog alarm with solar panels and batteries for power. The vinyl siding covering the tower indicates its modernity. This lighthouse shares with Peggy's Point a setting on a smoothly glaciated massive grey granite rock, but it is much less visited that its famous neighbour. The Betty Island's lighthouse now quietly shines its automated, unmanned light out over the Atlantic. It was still manned in 1981, when this photograph of the old classic lighthouse was taken. Access is by helicopter or boat.

Terence Bay

Grey granite rocks shaped during the Ice Age and endlessly washed by the sea form Nova Scotia's coastline south and west of Halifax. They are especially well known in the countless photographs of the Peggy's Point (Peggy's Cove) lighthouse on its smooth rounded point. At Terence Bay, a small upwardly tapering peppershaker lighthouse sits in the same type of granite setting, surrounded by the sea. It is unusual in that its lanternhouse was removed and replaced by an open red light when the lighthouse was automated and put on solar power very early in the modernization program.

It is sobering to think that one of the great shipwrecks of the 19th century occurred nearby. In 1873, the SS *Atlantic* sank after running onto the rocks, taking 535 people to their death. Nearly 300 of the dead lie in a nearby graveyard along the same road at Sandy Cove, commemorated with a granite obelisk and memorial tablets.

This beautiful part of the coastline is reached on a small side road, marked Sandy Cove, from the village of Terence Bay, itself on a branch road off Route 333, reached from Exit 2 on Route 103, west of Halifax.

SAMBRO ISLAND

The oldest-serving lighthouse in Canada stands on a glacially rounded granite island, south of the entrance to Halifax Harbour. In 1758, the Nova Scotia legislature provided for the construction of a lighthouse on Sambro Island by levying taxes on alcohol and passing ships. The provincial government even conducted a lottery the same year to raise money. The beacon of this 18-metre (59-foot) stone tower first shone forth over the shipwreck-strewn waters in 1760. Since then, it has continued to see its share of shipwrecks nearby, from small fishing boats to the 8,800-ton *Bohemian*, which was wrecked in 1920 on a reef just 1.5 kilometres (1 mile) away.

Within a decade of its construction, ship captains began to complain that the light was not clearly visible. In 1771, the nearby wreck of the HMS *Granby* sparked a crisis. Rules for keepers were tightened, and equipment was modified. Improved lamps were developed locally that did not cloud the lantern glazing.

In later years, the light source followed the usual evolution through different fuels, including the new kerosene derived from coal, the invention of Abraham Gesner, a Nova Scotian. Argand lamps, mantle-vapor lamps, and finally electrification followed.

In 1907, another 6 metres (20 feet) of height was added to the original 18-metre (59-foot) tower. A cladding of shingles protects the mortar in the original masonry from the salt spray of storms. In 1969, the beautiful old Barbier lamphouse and cap, with its first-order Fresnel lens, were replaced with angular aluminum top and rotating airport-type beacon. Its distinctive daymark is three red bands around its white tower, with a red lanternhouse. The original lens is on public view at the Maritime Museum of the Atlantic in Halifax.

The Sambro Island lighthouse has witnessed naval and mercantile history from the days of sailing ships to the present-day container vessels and cruise ships. Several old cannons still on the island bear witness to its strategic military importance in Canada's early history. Now giant container ships and sleek liners with navigational gear undreamed of a century ago only glance at Sambro as they pass. Nevertheless, after two and a half centuries, it remains a useful light to local traffic on this coast of islands and reefs, tricky currents, and Atlantic storms.

Sambro is accessible only by boat. In summer, boat tours from Ketch Harbour travel to the Island and its famous lighthouse. It can be glimpsed from the loop road through Sambro village and Ketch Harbour (Routes 306 and 349), directly south of Halifax.

Sambro Island.

Chebucto Head ▸

Chebucto Head lightstation, on the west side of the entrance to Halifax Harbour, bristles with antennas and masts—a complete range of modern aids to navigation. It is part of the Halifax control system, monitoring traffic in and out of this world-ranking port. Nowadays, with radio beacons, radar, and global positioning systems aboard ships of all sizes, the light and foghorn seem almost incidental.

During both world wars, thousands of ships assembled in Halifax Harbour and adjacent Bedford Basin, and passed by as they set out for Britain.

The first light on Chebucto Head was erected in 1872, following Sambro by more than a century. The modern reinforced concrete tower dates from 1977.

This station is readily accessible from Halifax via Purcell's Cove Road.

George's Island ▴

Now officially called the Halifax Harbour Inner Range, a lighthouse has stood sentinel on the shore of George's Island in Halifax Harbour since 1876. At present, it is a 17-metre (56-foot) octagonal tower with a red cap and bearing a fluorescent red vertical stripe on the seaward side. Nearby are the old fortifications, including a colonial walled fortress, complete with moat and gun emplacements from both world wars. The fort is now closed to the public, but Parks Canada plans to restore it and make it accessible once again.

The George's Island lighthouse is visible from the seaward end of the Historic Properties on the Halifax waterfront.

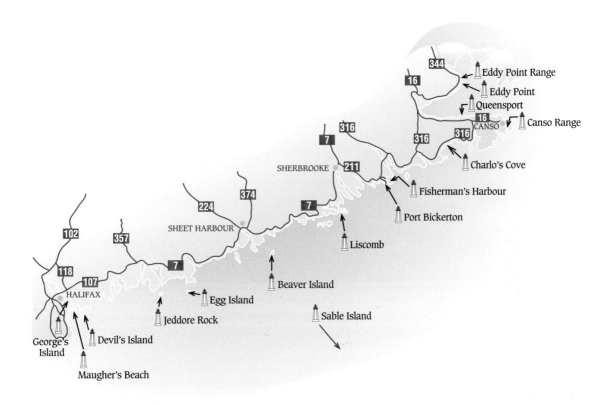

George's Island
Maugher's Beach
Devil's Island
HALIFAX
Jeddore Rock
Egg Island
Beaver Island
Liscomb
Sable Island
SHEET HARBOUR
SHERBROOKE
Port Bickerton
Fisherman's Harbour
Charlo's Cove
Queensport
Canso Range
CANSO
Eddy Point
Eddy Point Range

𝒯*he Marine Drive*
serves a less settled area than the adjacent Lighthouse Route.
The coastline is nevertheless spectacular with many capes and coves, and
hundreds of islands and shoals. Lighthouses serve coastwise vessels,
fishermen, and some passing deep-sea traffic offshore.

MAUGHER'S BEACH

For thousands of men sailing for Europe during both world wars, Maugher's Beach lightstation provided one of the last glimpses of land. Once a complete lightstation with keepers' houses, service buildings, and dock, the lighthouse now stands alone on its rock-ballasted point bearing little reminder of a history going back to 1814, when the military built a massive granite martello tower equipped with several defensive guns on the end of the spit.

In 1826, after marine interests demanded a light of some type here, the Nova Scotia legislature mounted a beacon on the existing stone tower to save money. The present concrete tower replaced it in 1941, but several years passed before the old stone martello tower and its foundations were removed. The foghorn was discontinued in 1993 after 104 years of sounding through Atlantic fogs.

The present octagonal reinforced concrete light tower is nearly 15 metres (49 feet) high. A flaring concrete platform supports an octagonal aluminum lamphouse with an automatic light.

Spits and sandbars such as Maugher's Beach are temporary structures by nature and subject to wave erosion, so, in 1987, Maugher's Beach spit was rebuilt and heavily ballasted with large rocks. The residence and other buildings were torn down at that time.

In 1851, Maugher's Beach lighthouse was witness to the first experiments using kerosene distilled from coal to fuel the lamps. The experiment was a great success, and the discovery of Abraham Gesner, a Nova Scotia physician and scientist, rapidly became the standard lighthouse fuel in Canada and many other countries. Kerosene lamps still burned in some small Canadian lightstations until the 1950s.

Maugher's Beach lighthouse is accessible by a small ferry that crosses from Eastern Passage to McNabb's Island. From there, footpaths lead to the site.

DEVIL'S ISLAND ▲

From the end of the road on Harlin Point, at the southeast side of Eastern Passage, southeast of Halifax, visitors can just see the decapitated light tower of the Devil's Island lightstation. It stands alone now with no service buildings and carries a flashing light on its old empty platform, with the sea all around and ships to the south and west heading in and out of Halifax Harbour.

Devil's Island is accessible only by boat or helicopter.

JEDDORE ROCK ▶

Some 30 kilometres (19 miles) east of Halifax, Jeddore Rock rises from the sea like an enormous stone whale. A square lighthouse station with a tower emerging from the centre of its roof, it has supplied direction to coastal shipping and fishermen since 1881. It is now automated and runs on solar power.

Jeddore Rock is accessible only by boat or helicopter.

EGG ISLAND ▸

A tiny rocky island off the coast of Nova Scotia about 55 kilometres (30 nautical miles) east of Halifax is crowned by a square skeleton tower with a central round core and a flashing light powered by solar panels on its flat platform. The 16-metre (53-foot) tower used to have a keeper's house nearby, but it now stands alone, in automated solitude, with only gulls and cormorants for company. Access is by boat or helicopter.

SABLE ISLAND ◂

Sable Island lies in the open Atlantic a little more than 315 kilometres (170 nautical miles) east-southeast of Halifax. This 34-kilometre (21-mile) -long island is a crescent-shaped deposit of sand and gravel left by glaciers 12 thousand years ago. Beyond each visible end, it extends for miles beneath the sea as shallows and reefs, and it has been a hazard to navigation since ships first crossed the Atlantic.

Sable Island has claimed literally hundreds of ships, the wrecks soon swallowed by the drifting sands, sometimes to be exhumed decades later by erosion. It is unknown how many vessels that sailed forth into the eastern Atlantic and were later reported as "lost with all hands" actually lie in these sands and in the shallows offshore.

Sable Island's lighthouse history dates from the 18th century, when concern grew over the number of ships lost nearby. By 1801, a modest lifesaving station had been established on the island. In those days, the argument still raged over whether a lighthouse would attract ships to their doom or warn them off. Finally, in 1873, lighthouses were built at each end of the island.

Erosion on the west end of the sandy island was severe, and from time to time, massive Atlantic storms removed hundreds of metres of land. Prior to 1940, the west lighthouse was moved six times for a total distance of almost 13 kilometres (8 miles). The east lighthouse has enjoyed a more stable existence. While it has been replaced several times, it remains on the original site. Both lighthouses were square towers with buttresses added for stability. Their lights were visible for more than 20 kilometres (12 miles). Today, a tall steel tower bears an automated revolving searchlight beacon.

Lighthouse keepers on Sable Island had remarkable company in the herd of wild horses that runs free on the beaches and among the sand dunes. The horses' ancestors either swam ashore from a shipwreck in the 18th century or were brought over about that time. They have adapted and maintain a population of about 250.

Nowadays, Sable Island is the scene of oil and gas exploration just offshore. It is restricted as an ecologically sensitive area because of its unusual flora and fauna and its herd of wild horses.

Beaver Island ▶

In 1846, a lighthouse was established on Beaver Island, the outermost in a cluster of islands off Sheet Harbour in Guysborough County. A strange-looking structure with its tower on one side of a two-storey residence and service buildings nearby, it was torn down in 1986 and replaced by a white circular fibreglass tower with an automated unmanned light.

Beaver Island is accessible only by boat or helicopter.

Liscomb ▼

Roughly halfway between Halifax and the Strait of Canso, at the west end of an island just off Liscomb on Nova Scotia's Guysborough County shoreline, stands a concrete tower with a red cap. The original tower was built in 1872, and the station has served coastwise traffic since then. Six-and-one-half kilometres (4 miles) to the east of Liscomb, the rusting remains of the *Fury* (left) has rested broadside to the Atlantic since she lost her steering and was driven aground in a storm in 1964. Access is by helicopter or boat.

The rusting hulk of the Fury, *swept aground in 1964.*

Port Bickerton

A classic example of a lighthouse mounted on the centre of a square residence is preserved on the end of Barachois Head, near Port Bickerton, on the eastern shore of Nova Scotia. It is located 16 kilometres (10 miles) southeast of Sherbrooke, the site of a restored historic village on principal Route 7. The original two-storey lighthouse has been completely renovated, and the operating light has been moved to a square service building nearby.

Visitors can climb into the lantern room in the old tower, now a viewing platform for the superb maritime scenery all around. Community volunteers run this station and charge an entrance fee. They have created a small museum with marine and lighthouse artifacts.

Of special note is a series of albums on display with photographs of almost all the lighthouses of Nova Scotia. The old keeper's house is now filled with models.

Turn off Route 7 onto Route 211 and go to Port Bickerton. From there, follow the Lighthouse Road for about 3 kilometres (2 miles) along the shore to the lightstation.

FISHERMAN'S HARBOUR ▲

As its name implies, Fisherman's Harbour is a rustic scene of wharves, fishing boats, lobster traps, and a classic peppershaker lighthouse on a spit near the dock, with the dark wooded shoreline in the background. From just east of Port Bickerton on Route 211, follow a branch road 4 kilometres (2.5 miles) to Fisherman's Harbour. Visitors should note that the coastal road is Route 211 west of Isaacs Harbour and Route 316 east of the village.

CHARLO'S COVE ▶

Between Port Bickerton and Charlo's Cove to the east, the marine drive encounters Country Harbour, a deep inlet. Travellers can either go north around it through Isaacs Harbour or cut across it on the ferry. Route 316 along the coast passes through Charlo's Cove, east of Port Bickerton and west of Canso. A lonely looking back range light on a side street is visible from the main road. It is a short four-sided pyramid with a square unlit lantern top.

It is the survivor of a pair built in 1901, with only the foundation of the front light on the end of the point. This fishing village, founded by Acadians to avoid expulsion troubles, is on a coast that has known commercial fishing since the mid 16th century. An attractive picnic area with beach and harbour view is on the waterfront.

Between Country Harbour and Canso the road parallels some of the wildest, unspoiled coastline in Nova Scotia. To savour it, look for the signs to Torbay Park en route and then walk the long sandy beaches, sand dunes and rocky headlands facing the open Atlantic.

Canso Range ◀

The village of Canso sits on a peninsula at the southeast corner of mainland Nova Scotia. In the early maritime history of eastern North America, its geographical position well out in the ocean made it a desirable location. One of the early 18th century settlements, on Grassy Island, just offshore, is now a national historic site.

The most accessible lighthouse is the rear range light just back of the hospital off Union Street. At the top of a hill a little farther along Union Street, near the last houses, is a view of the front range light down near the waterfront. From here, visitors can see other lights and former lights. Far out to sea, visible only in clear weather, is Cranberry Island light with its old square house and its light tower on the peak of the roof.

Canso is accessible from the Trans-Canada Highway (Route 104), via Route 16 south from Exit 37. As you enter the town of Canso, watch for Union Street and turn right toward the hospital and viewpoint. The Historic Sites office is along the way.

Queensport ▼

Route 16 becomes the shore road along the south side of Chedabucto Bay in the southeast corner of mainland Nova Scotia. At Queensport, you have a good view of a small rocky island with grass cover, crowned by a residence building and square lighthouse with its tower on the central peaked roof. This is a beautiful example of a lighthouse style common in the mid-18th century. Only a few examples are left, and Queensport is among the most accessible. Gilbert's Cove and Port Bickerton are other accessible examples in Nova Scotia. *(See pages 133 and 174.)*

Eddy Point ▲

Ships northbound for the Gulf of St. Lawrence along the Atlantic coast used to cut through Canso Strait between Cape Breton Island and mainland Nova Scotia to save many sea miles. Smaller ships are still able to use the canal lock that cuts through the causeway completed in 1955 across the strait.

A lighthouse was built in 1851 on the low sand and gravel spit of Eddy Point, on the south side of the Atlantic entrance to Canso Strait. In 1984, the lightstation consisted of a square tower with a square lanternhouse and a nearby keeper's house. It was replaced about 1988 by a round steel tower with a plain octagonal lanternhouse 8.5 metres (28 feet) tall. The rest of the station buildings were removed. In 2001, even this tower was removed. Now nothing remains of the station except part of the concrete foundation at waterline with its rusting ring of holding bolts.

The site is accessible from the Trans-Canada Highway by turning south on Nova Scotia 344 at Mulgrave. Go 14 kilometres (9 miles) to Sand Point, where a local road marked "Eddy Point Lighthouse" takes you to a spot gone back to nature.

Eddy Point Range ▶

The Canso Strait is sprinkled with range lights. The Eddy Point light is typical and located near the Eddy Point site described above.

New Brunswick Border to Canso

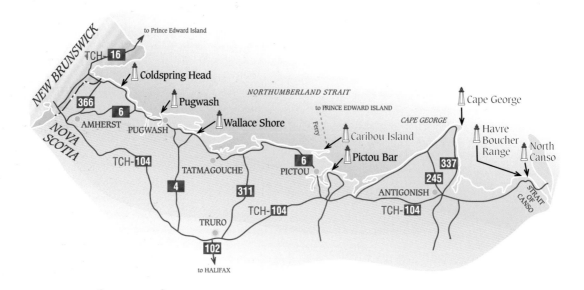

$\mathcal{T}$he Sunrise Trail,
Highway 6, serves the shoreline of Nova Scotia along the
Northumberland Strait, a partially protected waterway in contrast to the
open ocean of the south coast. The shore is notably shallow and sandy
near the New Brunswick border but marked by inlets and
many-armed bays farther east. Lighthouses
serve local fishermen and some
oceangoing traffic.

Coldspring Head ▶

The coastline of Nova Scotia east from the New Brunswick border is a continuation of the low sandy shore typical of adjacent New Brunswick, with small fishing ports at inlets here and there. Long beaches and warm water make the area popular with cottagers. The 11 metre (36-foot) -high tapering square white tower that stands on the rocky point of Coldspring Head supplies a landmark for fishermen and pleasure craft. Its lanternhouse is of the old-fashioned hexagonal type, with an emergency light on the balcony and a wind-driven ventilator on top.

Take Route 366 north from Amherst to the shore. Between Lorneville and Northport on Route 366, small roads lead to the shoreline. The road marked "Lane 26" takes you down to the Coldspring Head lighthouse.

Pugwash (Fishing Point) ◀

Pugwash is the shipping port for the salt mine that is visible from the main road, Route 6, where it crosses the inner harbour. Fishing Point is along the northeast corner of Pugwash Harbour and bears a skeleton tower with a white enclosed top that is some 15 metres (49 feet) high.

To view this interesting light, take the branch road off Route 6, opposite the Co-op store, and follow along the shore to a farm property with a lighthouse range marker in the field. Turn down the road around this property and continue until you see the light on stilts at the point. A lane leads to the cottages and the shore for a better view.

WALLACE SHORE AND MULLINS POINT

The village of Wallace is on Route 6, about halfway along the south shore of Wallace Harbour, a deep inlet from Northumberland Strait. Two of the several range lights that assist local marine traffic are readily accessible. Just west of the village, a branch road to the north crosses a highly visible bridge, just beyond which a road leads along the shore. Turn east and watch for the Mullins Point range light on the left. It is an unusual design with a large light tower protruding from the roof of a two-storey house (above).

Just east of Wallace on the main shore road, Route 6, stands an unusual little range light—a squat little peppershaker with two red bands below the platform on the seaward side and a strange lanternhouse (right).

Caribou Island

The ferry between Prince Edward Island and Nova Scotia passes near the lighthouse at the northeast tip of Caribou Island, near the entrance to Pictou Harbour. First built in 1868, the light-station is now a square white service building with a tower on the corner, capped with an octagonal red lanternhouse built in 1986. A bank of foghorns and some weather instruments complete the picture. The shallow waters make for pleasant beaches, but the area is susceptible to erosion, so the lighthouse station is partially protected by cribbing.

Take the shore road off from Route 6, the main coastal road west of Pictou, near Caribou River. Follow it about 6 kilometres (3.5 miles) to the Caribou Island Road turnoff, then about 10 kilometres (6 miles) to the lightstation at the end of the road. The coastal scenery—with its beaches, lagoons, sandbars, spits, and seabirds—makes this an interesting side trip. From the lightstation, visitors can often see the Prince Edward Island ferry on its several trips a day across the Northumberland Strait. The ferry operates seasonally from May to December.

PICTOU BAR

A lighthouse with a spectacular daymark stands on the end of Pictou Bar, providing guidance into Pictou Harbour. The lightstation, first established in 1834, is now an octagonal white tower nearly 15 metres (49 feet) high with each corner picked out in tapering vertical stripes in Coast Guard red. The red octagonal lanternhouse looks over the low coastline with its sandbars, islands, and spits at the entrance to the multi-armed Pictou Harbour, gateway and shipping port for the industrial area around Trenton, Stellarton, and New Glasgow.

Route 348 leads north from Trenton. The lighthouse at the end of the sandbar is visible just east of Pictou Landing. The 20-minute walk on the sandbar to the lighthouse is an experience in itself, with the wave-lapped beach, nesting terns, and wonderful scenery.

Cape George

The Sunrise Trail east from Pictou and Stellarton follows Route 245, then Route 337 around Cape George, an imposing headland on the west side of St. George's Bay. A solitary octagonal white lighthouse some 12.5 metres (41 feet) stands on the highest point, approximately 120 metres (394 feet) above the sea. A full station with residences and service buildings once stood where the modern concrete tower with its octagonal red lanternhouse and automated light was built in 1968. The third lighthouse to occupy this site, it was preceded by lighthouses constructed in 1861 and 1907.

The lighthouse commands an impressive view of St. George's Bay toward Cape Breton to the east, the open ocean to the north, and the dim outlines of Prince Edward Island to the northwest. It is located on Lighthouse Road, just off Route 337.

Nesting terns at Pictou Bar.

HAVRE BOUCHER RANGE

A short excursion via Exit 38 from Route 104 takes visitors into Havre Boucher. Direct access to these range lights is a little difficult because the upper light is surrounded by trees and backs onto a residential area, and the lower light on the shore is cut off by the railway yards. However, the lower range light, below and beyond the railway tracks at Havre Boucher, is readily visible from the Trans-Canada Highway, Route 104.

The lighthouses are standard wooden peppershaker towers with red tops and red vertical daymarks on their seaward sides. Their function since the mid-19th century has been to aid entry into the harbour from the fishing grounds of the Northumberland Strait and St. George's Bay.

North Canso

The North Canso lighthouse is not readily accessible, but it is visible across the Strait of Canso from points along Highway 19, a few kilometres north of the east end of the Canso Causeway. A private road leading to a cluster of cabins on a hillside, well visible from the main highway, provides a good vantage point. That tiny white structure against the dark land across the water is what the seaman sees when first coming into sight of land. In the days of manned lighthouses, the railway curving out around the cape was the only company that lighthouse keepers had.

Cape Breton Island

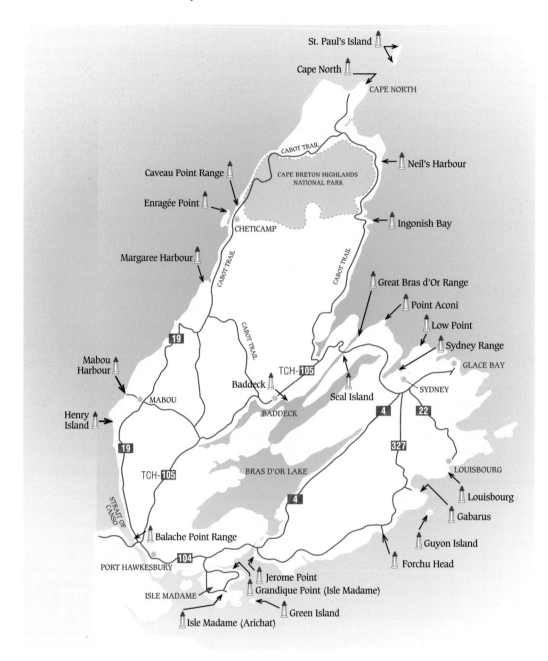

St. Paul's Island

Cape North

CAPE NORTH

CABOT TRAIL

Caveau Point Range

CAPE BRETON HIGHLANDS
NATIONAL PARK

Neil's Harbour

Enragée Point

CHETICAMP

Ingonish Bay

CABOT TRAIL

CABOT TRAIL

Margaree Harbour

Great Bras d'Or Range

Point Aconi

Low Point

19

Sydney Range

CABOT TRAIL

TCH-105

GLACE BAY

Mabou
Harbour

Baddeck

Seal Island

SYDNEY

MABOU

BADDECK

4

22

Henry
Island

327

19

BRAS D'OR LAKE

LOUISBOURG

TCH-105

Louisbourg

4

Gabarus

STRAIT OF CANSO

Balache Point Range

Guyon Island

PORT HAWKESBURY

104

Forchu Head

Jerome Point

ISLE MADAME

Grandique Point (Isle Madame)

Green Island

Isle Madame (Arichat)

*C*ape Breton Island, now
connected to the mainland by the Canso Causeway, has
a variety of shorelines from the low, much-indented southwest
half to the bold bluffs of the Highlands of the northwest. It is unusual in
marine terms in having the very large saltwater lakes of the Bras d'Or in the
interior. Its lighthouses are of different types to serve the deep-sea traffic
of the outside coasts, fishing villages, and the inside waters
of the well-travelled Bras d'Or Lakes.

Balache Point Range ▲

This small peppershaker tower with its square lamphouse and red vertical daymark stripe is visible from the Trans-Canada Highway at the Cape Breton end of the causeway that crosses the Strait of Canso.

To get close to the Balache Point range light, take the small driveway at the causeway end of the swing bridge. The scene is unusual in its clutter, with the lighthouse, swing bridge, causeway, and assorted transmission towers nearby. In season, you may notice the abundance of lobster trap buoys bobbing in the waters just off the rocky edges of the causeway. The canal through the causeway was built to compensate for the differences in tides on the two sides.

Grandique Point (Isle Madame) ▶

Picturesque fishing villages set in exceptional maritime scenery and a half dozen small lighthouses make an attractive side trip from the main roads of Cape Breton, east of Port Hawkesbury. From Route 104 at Louisdale, take Route 320 south and turn left around Isle Madame and its many scenic satellite islands toward Arichat, the principal village.

After approximately 10 kilometres (6 miles), watch for a small sign and turn into Lennox Passage Provincial Park. At the north end of the park, a wooden peppershaker lighthouse sits on a sandspit at Grandique Point. Its square platform supports a lamphouse with a fixed green light. The park is a pleasant spot with picnic tables, a swimming beach, and hiking trails in the woods.

Isle Madame (Arichat) ▶

At Arichat, the principal village on Isle Madame, views of the harbour with islands and a lighthouse at the end of the point remind visitors that this village, dating from the 1700s, was once a booming Atlantic seaport. Lower Road leads east from Arichat toward Petit-de-Gras, a fishing village with a history dating to 1500, when Basque and Portuguese fishermen took refuge there.

From Little Anse, a little farther on, a hiking trail leads to Cap Rouge and a view over the open sea to the lighthouse on Green Island. West from Arichat, on Route 320, visitors can see a lighthouse on Jerseyman Island on the north side of Arichat Harbour. It is a white tapering tower built in 1872 and now automated. At some points along this road, the lighthouse on Marache Point, on the south side of Arichat Harbour, may be visible in the distance in fine weather.

Jerseyman Island.

Green Island ▲

Several coastal lights mark the approaches to the Strait of Canso between Cape Breton Island and mainland Nova Scotia. The Green Island lighthouse, on the northeast side of Chedabucto Bay on the way into the Strait of Canso, faces the Atlantic to the southeast. Here, in a photograph taken in the 1980s, is the skeleton tower surrounding an enclosed stairwell. This was later replaced by a single white circular tower, automated with electronic horns. It also commands the entrance to the Bras d'Or Lakes via St. Peter's Bay.

The lightstation is visible from Cap Rouge beyond Little Anse on the tip of Isle Madame.

JEROME POINT ▶

The waters of the Bras d'Or Lakes from St. Peter's Bay were once separated by a narrow neck of land. This was a traditional portage route until the mid-19th century, when the St. Peter's Canal was cut through it. Tidal differences on the two sides necessitated the installation of a lock. In 1883, a lighthouse was built on the Atlantic end, and its fixed red beam still indicates the way into St. Peter's Canal. A tapering white wooden tower supports a bracketed platform and an octagonal lantern-house.

The Jerome Point lighthouse is off Route 104, where it crosses St. Peter's Canal in Battery Provincial Park, with its campground and picnic areas.

FORCHU HEAD ▶

A slender white tower about 10 metres (33 feet) high with two red bands shows a fixed white light on Forchu Head, on the southeast corner of Cape Breton Island. The fishing community of Forchu lies along Forchu Harbour, a protective inlet with Forchu Head on the south side. A small service building with fog horn attached is all that remains of the full station first built here in 1907. Concrete foundations show where the keeper's house and other buildings once stood.

Turn right off Route 4, just east of St. Peter's, on Route 247. After 13 kilometres (8 miles), turn left to Grand River, and there turn right over the bridge and follow the signs for Forchu along the coastal road. Continue through the village toward South Forchu on a gravel road for about 1.5 kilometres (1 mile). Just beyond the wharves, a break-water provides access to Forchu Head, with the light on the far side.

Guyon Island

In 1980, a short octagonal tower and red lamphouse replaced the original wooden structure on Guyon Island, off the southeast coast of Cape Breton Island, about 37 kilometres (20 nautical miles) southwest of Louisbourg. The flashing light and electronic horns are powered by solar panels. This photograh was taken in 1980, just before the lightstation was automated and left unmanned. Access is by boat or helicopter.

GABARUS

A well-marked side road, Highway 327, off the main Fleur de Lys Trail on Cape Breton Island, south of Sydney, leads to the fishing village of Gabarus. After about 4 kilometres (2.5 miles), the road turns right toward the main village. To the left, Harbour Point Road leads directly onto a flat gravelly area. At the far side, a rough road up a small hill brings visitors to the lighthouse just beyond the trees.

A square lighthouse tower about 9.5 metres (31 feet) tall with a red lanternhouse overlooks a rocky shoreline. To the right is a halfmoon bay with islands and the wharf area with its colourful fishing boats, fishing sheds, and the picturesque village. This is a lovely spot to picnic and enjoy beautiful seascapes.

LOUISBOURG

Prior to 1730, signal fires were lit on a point of land on the east side of Louisbourg Harbour, the site of a major French fortress. These proved to be unsatisfactory, so in 1731 the construction of a stone tower some 20 metres (66 feet) high was authorized by Louis XV. This, the first lighthouse of record in Canada, had a wooden light chamber on top with an open coal fire as the light. The wooden top, however, was soon destroyed by fire, and it was replaced by a masonry top with oil lamps. This lasted with various improvements until 1758, when British artillery put it out of commission. It was not replaced until 1842, when a new wooden lighthouse was built. This light lasted until the present octagonal reinforced concrete tower with an octagonal lamphouse was installed in 1923. It is unusual in its patterned concrete base and its sturdy concrete platform. Its diaphone of 1902 was replaced with electronic horns in 1972.

Plan, Profil et Elevation de la Tour proposée a faire sur la butte de l'Entrée du port de Louisbourg, qui servira a éclairer les Vaisseaux et les guider
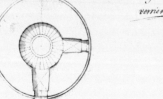
verney

Plans for a lighthouse at Louisbourg, begun in 1831.

The magnificent reconstructed fortress of Louisbourg is accessible by taking Exit 8 onto Route 22 off Route 162 at Sydney. At Louisbourg, a scenic drive along the northern shore of Louisbourg Harbour leads to Lighthouse Point. Old building stones and bits of ancient masonry around the base of the present lighthouse attest to the troubled history of the site. It is now a developed historic site with information panels and markers. In the midst of so much history, the bank of modern electronic foghorns looks odd.

Low Point

A major landfall light on Low Point at the east side of the entrance to Sydney Harbour is visible to thousands of passengers on the Newfoundland ferries every year. It stands on the easily eroded rocks of the local Coal Measures and is protected by a stone-filled cribbing along the shoreline. The tower is a fine reinforced concrete octagon about 20 metres (66 feet) high with a concrete base, plinth, and decorative corbel. Its sides flare out to the platform that supports a tall round lanternhouse of the old style with vertical rows of glass panes on ten sides. This photograph was taken when the magnificent Fresnel lens was still in place and the white tower had been stripped in preparation for repainting. The unmanned automated light is alone now with a modern bull's-eye lamp and electronic foghorn. Only foundations mark the locations of the former service buildings.

From Sydney, take the shore road, Route 28, north around the harbour to New Victoria. Look for Brown's Road and turn left. After about 3/4 of a kilometre (1/2 mile), turn right and continue for about the same distance, then turn left onto a dirt road. From here the lighthouse is visible. This spot is often foggy, but the trip is worthwhile to view this splendid 1938 lighthouse with its original form preserved.

Sydney Range (Point Edwards)

An impressive front range light sits on a point at the south side of Sydney Harbour's North West Arm. It is about 17 metres (56 feet) high, and with its tapering shingled sides, flared platform, and ten-sided lanternhouse, it looks more like a freestanding lighthouse than the typical range light. The neatly crafted windows on the outside indicate the different levels inside. Its bright orange vertical stripe on the seaward side is distinctive. The rear range light, a square tower about 12 metres (39 feet) high with the usual red daymark is set well back from the water and is less impressive.

Take Route 239 northeast from Exit 4 on Route 125 for about 6.5 kilometres (4 miles) to a narrow private lane leading to the light on the left and a residence on the right.

POINT ACONI

The area around Point Aconi lightstation reflects the history of early Cape Breton, when a vast quantity of coal mined nearby was converted into electricity. The Prince Mine had its pithead near the lightstation and followed the main coal seam deep below the light and out under the sea. Nearby are the remains of the huge ventilation system for the mine deep underground.

The lighthouse, a modern white circular metal tower, has an angular octagonal aluminum lamphouse with outward-sloping glass panes and an automated light. It is about 12 metres (39 feet) high and sits on a headland about 14 metres (46 feet) above the sea. A small service building stands near the tower. The setting is outstanding with the white and red lightstation in the midst of eroding cliffs of gently dipping bedded rocks, green slopes beyond the shore, islands, seabirds, wave wash, and the ocean to the far horizon.

Access is by Point Aconi Road, which leaves the Trans-Canada Highway, Route 105, near the western end of the bridge over the waterway just west of Exit 18. Follow the road to its end.

Bras d'Or Range

The seaward end of the long channel that connects the Bras d'Or Lakes with the open Atlantic is marked with range lights at Noir Point. The rear light is a tall tapering square tower with an orange vertical front stripe. It is visible through the trees and across a field from the end of the road at the old ferry dock.

Take Exit 14 from Highway 105 (marked Great Bras d'Or) and follow it along the shoulder of the ridge for about 6 kilometres (3.5 miles). Turn left onto Ferry Road for a short distance to the old ferry dock.

SEAL ISLAND (BOULARDERIE) ▲

On Cape Breton Island, the Trans-Canada Highway crosses the Great Bras d'Or Channel on the high span of the Seal Island Bridge. A clear view southwest from the bridge includes a small abandoned peppershaker-style lighthouse sitting on a superb example of a cuspate spit jutting out from the southeast shore.

It is accessible, with some difficulty, from a small side road at Exit 13 and then on foot, but this lighthouse is probably best left as a view from the bridge.

BADDECK (KIDSTON ISLAND) ▶

Baddeck, beloved summer home of Alexander Graham Bell, is on the Trans-Canada Highway in central Cape Breton at Exits 8 and 9. Its small harbour is protected by Kidston Island, on the northeast end of which sits a classic wooden lighthouse. Built in 1875 and modernized in 1984, it is still in seasonal service. This piece of traditional technology witnessed several pioneer Bell experiments. The *Silver Dart*, Bell's experimental aircraft, took off from the ice to make the first flight in the British Commonwealth. The first hydrofoil watercraft, also a Bell development, skimmed the local waters. Bell's home and the Bell Museum are landmarks in Baddeck.

The best view of the Kidston Island lighthouse is from the northeast end of Baddeck, in the dock and marina area, across from the Alexander Graham Bell Museum.

INGONISH BAY ▶ *No Longer there*

A tapering square lighthouse about 7.5 metres (25 feet) high functioned for nearly a century on the gravel bar on the south side of the entrance to Ingonish Harbour, just south of the southern boundary of Cape Breton Highlands National Park. Its functions have long since been taken over by a skeleton tower. The photograph shows the old light in about 1980, shortly before it was demolished in a storm, with a glimpse of the Keltic Lodge on the far headland.

The Ingonish Bay lighthouse is accessible on a short side road at Ingonish Ferry off the Cabot Trail on the east side of Cape Breton Island, not far south of the boundary of Cape Breton Highlands National Park.

NEIL'S HARBOUR ▲

Neil's Harbour is a small fishing village just outside the northeast corner of Cape Breton Highlands National Park. In sight of the main highway, the Cabot Trail, is a small peppershaker light tower. The old-style octagonal lanternhouse encloses a modest light used by local sea traffic. Its position on the highest local point—with the sea, harbour, and village surrounding it—makes it a popular choice for photographers.

Cape North

At least a million people a year pass by the red-and-white checkerboard Cape North tower and lighthouse in front of the National Museum of Science and Technology in Ottawa. Its third-order Fresnel lens now throws its rotating beam across the museum grounds instead of out over the sea at its former home on the shoreline at the foot of the high hills on the northern tip of Cape Breton Island.

When I was the director of that museum, I wanted to make a real lighthouse available to the people of Canada in a public place. As soon as the Coast Guard decided to replace the cast-iron tower at Cape North in 1978, a museum crew was dispatched to the site. A few weeks later, the veteran of 70 years on that lonely coast (and prior to that at Cape Race) had been disassembled and its lens and lights carefully packed. A team of tractor trailers, with bulldozers pushing from behind, then struggled up the primitive trail on the 300-metre (985-foot) climb to the highway above with a load of many tons of disasssembled parts.

Once back at the museum workshops, a new reinforced concrete light platform was designed and built to replace the original, which over the decades had been eaten away by salt spray. The lamphouse had to be refurbished and painted, the lens and rotating gear cleaned and repaired, and a dozen or so new matching stanchions for railings cast at a local foundry.

In the spring of 1979, the new base was ready and the two-ton curved plates began to be reassembled. The new concrete platform was lowered by crane onto the tower. Then the lamphouse, the lenses, and the light were installed. The checkerboard pattern of red and white squares, its original daymark, was carefully repainted. Huge limestone blocks were arranged to give the impression of a lighthouse on an island, albeit in a sea of grass.

Now, in the nation's capital city, thousands of visitors troop through a real lighthouse steeped in maritime history. Additional thousands of passersby see its rotating Fresnel lens flashing atop its red and white tower every day.

Meanwhile, its old location is accessible for hardy hikers who are willing to walk down the steep rough road beyond Bay St. Lawrence at the tip end of Cape Breton Island and along the shore to the remnants of the station, now a modest automated light on a plain wooden tower. *(See page 127 for a view of the light just prior to its move to Ottawa.)*

The Cape North lighthouse during installation at the National Museum of Science and Technology, Ottawa.

St. Paul's Island

On a fine summer's day with calm seas and gentle breezes, a helicopter brought me to St. Paul's Island, off the tip of Cape Breton Island. As I surveyed the tranquil scene, I tried to imagine the place as T.H. Tidmarsh, a Nova Scotia lighthouse commissioner, had described it in 1833:

> Our route . . . gave us a melancholy view of the numerous wrecks with which the shore is strewed, the whole coast is covered with pieces of the wreck of ships. . . . The number of graves bore strong testimony also that some guide or land mark was wanting in the quarter to guard and direct the approach of strangers to this boisterous, rugged shore.
> (After Bush, E.L., 1975, p. 39)

Tragedy fills this area's history. In 1833, 10 ships went down off the outer shores of Cape Breton Island and 603 people perished. In 1834, the *Astrea* crashed ashore with 240 lost. When the *Sibylle*, with 316 aboard, sank off St. Paul's with all hands lost, there was a public outcry. Some of the *Jessie's* 27 passengers and crew struggled ashore after the ship foundered there. They left notes before dying

of starvation weeks later. After more years of debate on who would pay for a light, a financial arrangement was finally reached. In 1839, two lights were finished and lit, one at each end of St. Paul's.

The original lighthouses were tapering octagonal wooden buildings 12 metres (39 feet) high on 1.5 metres (5 feet) of stonework and equipped with polygonal iron lanterns with flat glass panes. In 1914, the south-end light was completely destroyed by fire. Its place was taken in 1916 by a stumpy round cast-iron tower only 3.5 metres (12 feet) high carrying a 3-metre (10-foot) polygonal lamphouse with a flashing petroleum vapor lamp (left). Eighty-five years later, it is still there. On the north end, the original light tower was replaced in 1962 by a standard reinforced concrete tower, described in the Canadian Coast Guard *List of Lights* as 14.6 metres (48 feet) high with its light about 42 metres (138 feet) above the water (above).

The islands are just visible as a smudge on the horizon from the highland on the tip of Cape Breton Island above Cape North. Access is very difficult and only by sea or air.

Caveau Point Range ▲

A standard tapering square wooden tower was built here in 1897 to serve as the rear range light for Cheticamp Harbour, in the heart of Acadian Cape Breton. At the northern end of the village, close to the main Cabot Trail, its neatly shingled sides bear a bright orange vertical stripe, the daymark, below a plain square lamphouse. A square seaward window shows a red light. Its front range counterpart, much closer to the water, is now a skeleton tower. Cheticamp, though popular with tourists, retains its fishing village character on the waterfront, and this lighthouse, along with the one at the end of the island across the water, is very much a part of the ambience.

Enragée Point (Cheticamp Island) ▲

A concrete hexagonal tower with a red angular lamphouse was constructed on the northwest portion of Cheticamp Island in 1938. About 12 metres (39 feet) high, it is a landmark for shipping in the Gulf of St. Lawrence and a marker for Cheticamp Harbour. Formerly a full lightstation with residences, it has recently been reduced by automation to a tower and lone service building.

The lighthouse is visible across the harbour from several places along the Cheticamp shore. It is accessed via the Cheticamp Island Road from the Cabot Trail. On the island, turn right onto a road along the shore. The area is a cooperative pasture, so obtain permission before going through the gated fence to the lightstation.

MARGAREE HARBOUR ▲

Two small peppershaker range lights of a routine kind mark the way into Margaree Harbour on the west side of Cape Breton, where the Cabot Trail turns inland to Baddeck. Each bears as a daymark the typical vertical orange stripe from ground to lanternhouse.

Margaree Harbour is accessible off Route 219 via the Shore Road to the breakwater area.

MABOU HARBOUR ▶

A tapering white tower, its concrete base at water's edge, rises some 12 metres (39 feet) above the sea at the government wharf in quite a lovely setting at Mabou Harbour. Its square red lanternhouse shows a fixed yellow light in its plain square glass windows. It was built in 1884 as the rear range light for Mabou Harbour, with the front light located some 600 metres (1970 feet) to the seaward side.

The lighthouse setting makes this a worthwhile side trip of roughly 7 kilometres (4.5 miles) on the Mabou Harbour Road, off the Ceiligh Trail, Route 19. It is an exceptionally interesting spot with a beautiful view, an interesting dock and lighthouse area, and a background of white gypsum knobs and cliffs in bumpy terrain. Lobster boats come and go in season, and groups of fishermen collect on the dock below the lighthouse to share stoies of tides and currents, the state of the fishery and markets, and local politics.

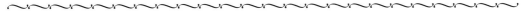

HENRY ISLAND

As you pass Port Hood on Route 19 along the coast of Cape Breton, note that an interesting lighthouse sits on Henry Island, the smaller of two islands about 5 kilometres (3 miles) offshore. It was built in 1901 to mark the eastern limits of St. George's Bay and the route into the Strait of Canso, thus complementing the light on Cape George on the western side *(see page 183)*.

The Henry Island lighthouse is located on a high point on the seaward side of the island. It is a tapering octagonal pyramid that flares out to a platform bearing a lamphouse with 16 windows and a solar panel for power. Its striking daymark has alternating white and red vertical panels that continue upward to include the platform edge. Its light is now automated and reduced to a 10-kilometre (6-mile) range from its former 30-kilometre (19-mile) range. The site is now privately owned, except for the lighthouse and an attendant service shed, with the keeper's house restored and nicely maintained.

The Nova Scotia Lighthouse Preservation Society, which runs occasional excursions to this lighthouse, may be contacted at the Nova Scotia Museum in Halifax.

Cape Race lightstation, Newfoundland.

Lighthouses
of
Newfoundland

Newfoundland is a place of great maritime beauty with nearly 50,000 kilometres (31,000 miles) of shoreline and thousands of bays and coves. But, for ships at sea, it can equally be a place of great savagery with its abrupt cliffs, offshore islands and ledges, impenetrable fogs, and legendary Atlantic storms. Since the 1400s, the banks around Newfoundland have attracted fishermen from Europe. In these earlier times, ships sailed under wind power and were subject to unknown currents and storms that sent them hundreds of kilometres off course. It is little wonder, then, that, as ships neared these shores, they encountered trouble along the unmarked coasts.

After the earliest visits by Spanish, Portuguese, and Basque fishermen in the 1400s, marine traffic gradually increased. By 1700, veritable armadas sailed from Europe each spring to fish the banks off Newfoundland and Labrador. Settlement was at first prohibited for political reasons, but, as fishermen began wintering in sheltered coves in remote places, settlement commenced. By the early 1800s, local traffic and passing ships en route to central Canada and the American seaboard intensified the need for lights.

Newfoundland's bold headlands, irregular islands, and reefs have a unique geological history. A thousand million years ago, all the planet's landmasses were joined in one giant continent. Its slow breakup and the subsequent movements of the earth caused the Atlantic Ocean to open and close three times, each time welding pieces of continental crust and enormous chunks of ocean bottom onto the eastern edge of North America. Glaciation and flooding by rising sea levels completed the complicated outlines of Newfoundland visible today.

Newfoundland's lighthouses are located in a unique setting of deep bays and inlets. The first light in Newfoundland was installed at Fort Amherst, St. John's, in 1813. Another major light was built at Cape Spear in 1834–35 and first lit the following year. Throughout the 1830s, shipping companies, the Royal Navy, and coastal schooner owners pleaded in London for the construction of more lights. During 1839, Newfoundland's first government geologist, J.B. Jukes, was caught in a hurricane gale, and the shoreline was littered with the wrecks of a dozen ships. Jukes was so moved by the loss of life and property that he recorded in his official record:

I should be unwilling to obtrude my opinion on matters of which I have no professional, and but little practical, knowledge: but surely it seems reasonable that a great commercial nation such as England should not suffer the borders of the great high-road to Canada and her North American possessions to be thus strewed with the properties and bodies of her subjects. A lighthouse on Cape Ray, with a large bell or gun to be used in fogs, together with a smaller lighthouse and a pilot or two, either at Port aux Basques, the Dead Islands, or La Poile, as a harbour of refuge, would be the means of great good.

–J.B. Jukes, 1842, Vol. 2, p. 187.

Finally, the pleas for help were heard, and more lights began to appear at several places, beginning with Cape Bonavista in 1843. In those days, the construction of aids to navigation required cooperation between London, the Royal Navy, the Government of Canada, the Newfoundland Assembly, and local merchants, so it is understandable that matters of jurisdiction delayed some lights. Nevertheless, the coastline and small ports slowly became well marked. In the modern Canadian Coast Guard List of Lights, some 550 sites are described, from one of the world's great lighthouses at Cape Race to local markers at small outports.

Lighthouses of Newfoundland

Belle Isle North
Belle Isle South
Cape Bauld
Cape Norman
ST. ANTHONY
Amour Point
430
Greenly Island
Flower's Cove
New Ferolle
Pointe Riche
Flat Island
St. Mary Islands (Îles Ste. Marie)
Lobster Cove Head
Woody Point
Trout River
430
Gull Island
Long Point (Twillingate)
Offer Wadham
Change Island
Puffin Island
GANDER
TCH-1
NEWFOUNDLAND
CORNER BROOK
Cape Bonavista
Heart's Content
Hant's Harbour
Brigus
Bell Island
Cape St. Francis
ST. JOHN'S
80
70
210
Fort Amherst
Cape Spear
Bull Head (Bay Bulls)
Cape Anguille
PORT AUX BASQUES
TCH-1
Cape Ray
Rose Blanche Point
Channel Head
100
10
Ferryland Head
Cape Race
to NOVA SCOTIA
220
Cape St. Mary's
Cape Pine
LABRADOR
QUEBEC
STRAIT OF BELLE ISLE
GULF OF ST. LAWRENCE

*B*ecause of the island's rugged
coastline, many lighthouses are located on offshore islands and remote
capes accessible only by boat or helicopter. Among those described in this chapter,
some are accessible, particularly on the Avalon Peninsula and along the
west coast. Others are included because of their importance to
navigation, their place in history, or their
unique character.

Belle Isle South

Ships from Europe bound for ports in the St. Lawrence have a choice of routes. One follows the great circle to just south of the landfall light at Cape Race on the southeast corner of Newfoundland, where it turns west through the Cabot Strait and into the Gulf of St. Lawrence. Another passes to the north of Newfoundland, through the Strait of Belle Isle, and into the Gulf.

The south end of Belle Isle was a logical place to build the first light for the northern route, and a spot was selected on a headland some 130 metres (427 feet) above the sea. Building materials had to be landed and then hauled up the frightening slopes. By 1858, a stone tower faced with fire-brick, later sheathed and shingled, was in service (above), but it was inadequate because of the area's many days of dense fog. Often the light shone bravely, but it was high above the weather, out of sight for ships.

In 1880, the problem was solved by constructing a second light on a lower site about 35 metres (115 feet) above the water (right). It was thus visible under most fogs. The standard round red lamphouse is set directly on a flat concrete base with no tower at all, making it one of the shortest lighthouses in Canada.

This wonderful lightstation, set on a spectacular barren site on the south end of Belle Isle, is accessible only by sea or helicopter.

Belle Isle North ▸

Because some ships pass into the Gulf of St. Lawrence by the route to the north of Belle Isle, in 1905, a second lightstation was installed on the north end of the island. Originally of cast iron, it was encased in concrete in 1908 and equipped with the flying buttresses developed by Colonel W.D. Anderson of the Canadian lighthouse service. It is topped by a red lanternhouse and has a distinctive beaver weather vane.

Like the south-end station, the north island lighthouse is remote and accessible only by air or sea. Both Belle Isle lightstations are now nominally maintained as seasonal lights from May to November.

Cape Norman ▾

Although lighthouses had been placed on the north side of the Strait of Belle Isle at Amour Point in 1855 and Belle Isle South in 1858, beacons were needed on the northern tip of Newfoundland to bracket the entrance to the Gulf of St. Lawrence. In 1871, a lightstation was built at Cape Norman.

A white wooden tower with a red rounded lamphouse and a Fresnel lens stood on the limestone cape with its residence and service buildings until it was replaced in 1980. Today, little is left at the old station except a white octagonal concrete tower about 15 metres (49 feet) high with the typical flared-out platform and the modern angular eight-sided lanternhouse. In 1971, an electronic horn replaced the original foghorn from 1880.

The principal road up the west side of the Northern Peninsula, Route 430, has several branch roads near its northern end. One of these, Route 435, with a marked side road, leads to Cape Norman. Another road leads to L'Anse aux Meadows and a restored 1,000-year-old Viking settlement.

Cape Bauld

Cape Bauld's red and white octagonal tower took its place on the outer end of Quirpon Island, at the northeast tip of Newfoundland, in 1884. Its purpose was to help bracket the Strait of Belle Isle opposite Belle Isle South. Its 1951 diaphone sent out its two-second blast every 20 seconds until the usual electronic replacement in 1971 and later automation. The rusting remains of a large freighter that was literally thrown onto Great Sacred Island, a few kilometres to the west, are testament to the might of winter storms in this dramatic location.

The keeper's residence next to the lighthouse has been converted into an inn. Now the lonely lighthouse is a popular centre for whale-watching, iceberg-watching, and sea kayaking along a spectacular coast and the islands to the west. It is directly accessible only by sea or helicopter. The inn picks up its visitors from the village of Quirpon, not far off the main route to the Viking settlement at L'Anse aux Meadows on Route 436.

Wreck on Great Sacred Island.

Gull Island

Gull Island, 8 kilometres (5 miles) off Cape St. John on the north coast of Newfoundland, has a special fascination for me. For two summers, it was a frequent sight as I walked and mapped the Cape's rocky shores as part of my doctoral thesis.

On a calm late summer's day, I leaped ashore from a small fishing boat from the top of a gentle Atlantic swell onto the one accessible ledge on Gull Island and then climbed the steep path to the top. On that beautiful day, it was difficult to realize that Gull Island was the scene of great storms and several tragic shipwrecks. The numerous braces and wire stays on the lighthouse buildings and the covered walkways are testament to winds of well over 120 kilometres (75 miles) per hour that blow in this exposed and barren place.

The first lighthouse was built here in 1884 and rebuilt in 1980. Distinctive features include its daymark of red and white vertical stripes and the uncommon triangular pattern of lamphouse glass. The light stands atop a tall bare rock some 150 metres (492 feet) above the sea. A diaphone horn, installed in 1918, was replaced with electronic horns in 1980.

What a lonely voice that old diaphone must have been out there all alone in the open ocean.

This lighthouse is not readily accessible, but from the high plateau northeast of La Scie, it is visible on the horizon. La Scie is on Route 440, a branch from Route 410, that leaves the Trans-Canada highway between Grand Falls and Deer Lake.

Long Point (Twillingate) ▶

On Long Point, on North Twillingate Island, a red concrete tower, boxy and square in shape with beveled shoulders and deep-set windows, supports a lamphouse with a railed concrete platform and a pattern of triangular window panes. This rugged place on Newfoundland's north coast required covered walkways between buildings to protect keepers in howling Atlantic gales. Its original Fresnel lens of 1876 was replaced with the usual rotating bull's-eye searchlight in 1980. It is listed as being about 9 metres (30 feet) high and 100 metres (328 feet) above sea level. Its half-second flash can be seen every six seconds from many kilometres out in the Atlantic.

This lightstation is accessible from Twillingate on Route 340, which leaves the Trans-Canada Highway between Glenwood and Norris Arm.

Rugged Twillingate shoreline.

Change Island ▶

For a few of weeks in August 1948, I was part of a three-man mapping crew that lived in tents beside the lighthouse at the southern tip of Change Island, on Newfoundland's north coast. No one else lived within 15 kilometres (9 miles), so we got to know the lighthouse keeper and his family well. My lasting memory is of one evening at dusk when the keeper left our conversation group to "light the lamp," which was wick and kerosene.

Now the point is empty, and the station is a white skeleton tower about 3 metres (10 feet) high, sitting about 14 metres (46 feet) above the sea. Its three seaward faces display white daymarks against the white skeleton.

Change Island is accessed from the ferry at Farewell, off Newfoundland Route 335.

The original lightstation at Change Island.

Offer Wadham ◂

A cluster of islets at the northeast corner of Newfoundland once had two remote lighthouses, one on Peckford Island and another on nearby Offer Wadham Island. The latter is included here as an example of a remote station in the middle of the ocean. Its original lightstation, a wooden house and tower built in 1858, was replaced in 1980 with a standard concrete tower and modern lamphouse. Now even that has been replaced with a skeleton tower and automated light.

In 1946, I came to Offer Wadham all the way from Fogo Island across the open Atlantic in a small trap skiff. This lightstation has always had a special fascination for me because of its location in the middle of the Labrador Current, which sweeps down from the north. In spring, it carries pack ice with thousands of seals and a flotilla of beautiful white icebergs that usually steal silently past—but not always. Every once in a while, an iceberg goes aground with great booming sounds, while shedding thousands of fragments that sound like tinkling xylophone notes. Offer Wadham is accessible only by air or sea.

Puffin Island ▲

The northeast corner of Newfoundland between Cape Freels and Cape Bonavista is one of Canada's most irregular coastlines with its thousands of islands, long headlands, and deep inlets. One of hundreds of aids to navigation that service the myriads of straits, channels, and tickles (small water passages between islands) is located on Puffin Island, a speck of land about halfway down the coast and exposed to the open Atlantic. While the lighthouse tower is a typical peppershaker with a standard four-sided wooden pyramid and a simple square-paned lanternhouse, its daymark is unique. The single red band on the white tower is common, but the concrete foundation is a pale blue-grey. The same pattern is applied to the residence, the service building, and the fog alarm house.

Offshore and accessible only by sea, the Puffin Island lighthouse is one of the few lightstations in Canada still manned.

Cape Bonavista

Long headlands and deep bays mark the northeast shore of Newfoundland. Cape Bonavista became an early major turning point for coastal navigation around the north coast, so a large light was placed here in 1843. It soon became a landfall light for ships from Europe.

A large square building with living quarters for the keepers was combined with a light tower in the centre of the peaked roof. Fortunately, the old station has been preserved, complete with its array of metre-wide reflectors and inset lamps, and it is now part of a provincial historic park. Nearby, a modern skeletal steel tower with a rotating airport-style beacon performs the lighthouse duties. Lightning set the old building afire in 1999, but it has been restored.

The white building is painted in broad red vertical stripes with a large red-trimmed light cupola on top. Inside are the living quarters and the massive central brickwork that housed the oven, stoves, and chimney. The original lamp system, brought from the famous Bell Rock lighthouse after having served shipping off the east coast of Scotland for many years, is kept in gleaming condition.

The station is readily accessible by taking Route 230 from the Trans-Canada Highway near Clarenville.

One of the multiple reflectors at Cape Bonavista.

Heart's Content ◄

The small harbour lighthouse at Heart's Content in Trinity Bay has a spiral daymark in red and white, very unusual in Canadian lighthouses. This short round tower stands about 7 metres (23 feet) tall and was built near the turn of the century. Heart's Content is famous as the eastern end of the early trans-Atlantic cables.

Take the Trans-Canada Highway west of St. John's to Route 80.

Hant's Harbour ▶

Another 20 kilometres (12 miles) north along Route 80 from Heart's Content brings vistitors to Hant's Harbour, where a white shingled tower about 6 metres (20 feet) high is located on a rocky prominence on the east side of the harbour. It is a tapering white, shingled tower on a square base that supports a well-bracketed octagonal platform and top. Triangular window panes and a conical red roof on the lamphouse give it a distinctive appearance. The lighthouse started life in 1881 with oil lamps but is now an automatic electric beacon visible for about 8 nautical miles. It is useful to local traffic along this rocky coast noted for its crab fishery.

Leave the main road for the harbour area and watch for trails leading down the east side.

Brigus

The west side of Conception Bay, south and west from Bell Island, was settled in a string of maritime villages beginning in the early 1600s. One of these is Brigus, a principal fishing and sealing port in its heyday during the 19th century and homeport to Captain Bob Bartlett, a prominent figure in arctic exploration.

The round cast-iron lighthouse, placed on North Head at the north side of the entrance to Brigus Bay in 1885, still functions, although other buildings were removed in the 1930s. It is marked on the seaward side by red and white vertical stripes, in contrast to the horizontal red strips on another tower of similar style located about 7 kilometres (4 miles) north at the south side of the entrance to Bay Roberts, on the west shore of Conception Bay.

Both lighthouses are accessible from the sea and with some effort on trails by land. Both Brigus and Bay Roberts can be reached from St. John's by the Trans-Canada highway and by following the clearly marked roads north along the west side of Conception Bay.

Bell Island

A superbly kept lighthouse is located on the northeast end of Bell Island in Conception Bay, 5 kilometres (3 miles) offshore from Portugal Cove. Bell Island is composed of the youngest rocks on the Avalon Peninsula, reddish sandstone and shale of Ordovician Age (about 450 million years ago) with several beds of iron ore. These were mined until 1966. In the heyday of mining during the 1940s and 1950s, Bell Island produced as much as a million tons of hematite ore a year, which was shipped all over the world. In 1940, early in the Second World War, near the docks on the southeast side, four ships were torpedoed leaving 69 people dead.

Even with large freighters coming and going, no lighthouse was built here until late 1940. Remodeled about 1980, the lighthouse now consists of a square tower on the corner of a single-storey service building. The keeper's house is nearby. Remains of older buildings are evident in the "ghosts" of foundations in the grass.

The light is a fixed omnidirectional lens of the third order with a flashing sequence. Power comes from Bell Island hydro mains, supplied in turn by submarine cable from Portugal Cove. The lanternhouse is an octagonal aluminum-frame type with flat glass windows. The electronic foghorn stands on the building's seaward side. Inside, the compressor and air tank for the old foghorn are kept in beautiful order by the caring keeper, whose pride in his station is clearly shown by the nicely kept garden and lawns.

Frequent ferry service and good roads on the island make this beautiful station easily accessible. From St. John's, take Portugal Cove Road to the ferry and then follow the marked local road to the north end of the island.

Islands and icebergs off the Cape.

CAPE ST. FRANCIS

The Cape St. Francis lighthouse is located on the northeast tip of the Avalon Peninsula. The original light was installed in 1887 for coastal shipping between St. John's and the northeast coast and Labrador. It was rebuilt in 1957 with the last full station arrangement added in 1980. The 1935 diaphone foghorn was replaced in 1971 with a bank of electronic horns. For many years, the old steam boiler for the foghorn sat forlornly beside its electronic successor, just below the light. A plain aluminum lamphouse, with no tower of its own, used to sit directly on the balcony of a white square residence and service building.

When the building was torn down, a helicopter pad was installed over the old foundation walls. The automated light, with an omnidirectional beam, sits atop it. In 1942, according to an eyewitness who had been a schoolboy on the station at the time, a sea battle between German U-boats and Allied corvettes took place within sight of the lightstation.

The station is now securely fenced and feels cold and friendless. No one watches the procession of icebergs drifting down in spring and summer or sees the ships passing beyond the nearby reefs where winter storms rage in the open Atlantic.

Cape St. Francis is about an hour's drive north of St. John's on Route 20, beyond the end of the pavement at Pouch Cove.

Lamphouse at Cape St. Francis.

Helicopter landing pad on old foundation.

Fort Amherst

Each year thousands of tourists visit Signal Hill and Cabot Tower on the north side of the narrow entrance to St. John's Harbour. From there the Fort Amherst lighthouse station is visible on the tip of South Head opposite. This region has a colourful history, with Cabot Tower, the old magazine, 18th-century cannons, the Battery site, and the remains of Second World War gun emplacements on both sides of the harbour entrance.

Portuguese fishermen came to these shores half a century before Columbus first arrived in the Caribbean. By 1700, cannon and lookouts had been placed on the point of the southern head at the entrance to St. John's Harbour with the main fortifications farther in. Until 1772, these guns alternately served French and English military masters as European wars spilled over into North America, and Newfoundland changed hands several times. In 1777, the fort and battery were completed by William Amherst and named Fort Amherst for his brother, Jeffery, who had lead English troops to victory at Louisbourg in 1773.

The first formal lighthouse in Newfoundland was established here in 1813, when a tower with an oil lamp was placed on top of the fort's stone barracks. In 1852, a triple-wick Argand lamp with an annular lens was installed—the first dioptric light in Newfoundland. During the First World War, some minor fortifications were added, but in the Second World War, heavy gun emplacements were built below the light, and some still remain. The present tower was completed in 1951, but public outcry stopped all work when its predecessor was scheduled to be demolished. For three years, two lighthouses stood at Fort Amherst, but in 1955 the old stone buildings and the original light were quietly removed.

The Fort Amherst lighthouse shares with the Estevan Point lighthouse on the west coast of Vancouver Island the rare distinction of having been directly fired on during the Second World War. In 1941, from just offshore, U-boat 587 fired two torpedoes at the St. John's Harbour entrance. One of these exploded on the rocks just below the guns but did no more than throw up a huge cloud of salty spray and startle the garrison.

The lighthouse is readily accessible from the St. John's South Side dock area and a footpath. This site also features superb maritime scenery, a rich history, and a tearoom in one of the former keeper's cottages.

CAPE SPEAR

In 1836, a large square building with a cupola on top was completed at Cape Spear, the easternmost point of North America. It was equipped with seven Argand lamps and reflectors that had earlier served at the Inchkeith lighthouse on the Scottish coast. The Cape Spear light's location on the point more than 70 metres (230 feet) above the sea made it visible for 33 kilometres (18 nautical miles) on clear nights.

This beautiful example of an 1830s lighthouse has been restored, although without the old lamps, and is maintained as a national historic site by Parks Canada. The duties of this long-retired dignified old lady of lighthouses are now performed by an octagonal concrete tower with an angular aluminum lamphouse and a rotating bull's-eye searchlight closer to the end of the point. Gun emplacements and barracks for the crews, installed below the lighthouse during the Second World War, are accessible along park footpaths.

Historic original Cape Spear lighthouse.

One of the remarkable light-keeping families of Newfoundland started at Cape Spear not long after the light was first built. One day in July 1835, the frigate *Rhine*, in the midst of the usual summer fog that shrouds the coast, could not find the entrance to St. John's Harbour. Eventually, a local man, James Cantwell, who dreamed of being a lightkeeper, located the vessel, and guided it to safety. Unknown to Cantwell, Prince Henry of Orange was aboard. He was so grateful that he arranged for Cantwell to get his wish to become the keeper of the light being constructed at the time on Cape Spear. When the position became vacant, he became the first of several successive generations of Cantwells to keep the light at Cape Spear, a record seldom matched.

From the upper end of St. John's Harbour, Route 11 leads up and over the hills directly to Cape Spear and the historic lightstation.

The rocky coastline near Cape Spear.

Bull Head (Bay Bulls) ▶

A slender slightly tapering white steel tower stands near the outer end of the north side of Bull Head on the north, some 25 kilometres (15 miles) south of St. John's. Its platform is an open metal grating with steel brackets, and the light is housed in a white octagonal lamphouse with flat panes and a ventilator-capped dome.

It can be reached by taking the road along the north side of Bay Bulls Harbour off Route 10, the coastal road south from St John's, and following it out the north side to the end of the road. From there, a walk of a little more than an hour along a partly developed pathway brings visitors to the lighthouse.

The area is interesting in summer, when boat tours leave Bay Bulls and Witless Bay to view icebergs in early summer, sea life such as whales and porpoises, and the bird islands of the Witless Bay Ecological Reserve. The stars there are the parrotlike puffins nesting in thousands. *(See also listing for Machias Seal Island, New Brunswick, page 68.)*

Ferryland Head ◀

The original tower on Ferryland Head, 75 kilometres (47 miles) south of St. John's, was built of brick in 1871. It was later sheathed in steel plates, so it looks somewhat similar to the real cast-iron lights that were prominent in Newfoundland during the late 19th century. The keeper's house was joined to the tower at the same time. Long since automated and on domestic hydro, the old light stands firm, but the residence has regrettably been vandalized. The triangular glass panes in the lamphouse are distinctive in the impressive old tower.

Ferryland is a wonderfully historic place. In the summer of 1621, George Calvert, later Lord Baltimore, landed here with a party of settlers to establish a colony. After years of poor weather, crop failures, and harassment from the sea, he left for the eastern United States, where he founded Maryland, named for his wife, and the city that bears his name. Archaeological investigations are now a feature of the old Calvert site just below the main road in Ferryland.

The Ferryland Head lighthouse is accessible by following the shore road, Route 10, south from St. John's to Ferryland and east along the sandbar to the visible headland. The last kilometre (0.6 mile) of the road is in very poor condition, so walking is recommended.

CAPE RACE

Cape Race, at the extreme southeast corner of Newfoundland, has long been the first land typically sighted by mariners on their way from Europe to Canada and the eastern seaboard of the United States. The cape appears on 16th-century maps as *Cabo Raso*, Portuguese for "flat cape." Cape Race is one of the most interesting lighthouses anywhere for its spectacular geographic location, its history of shipwrecks and bravery, and its sheer size and power. We are fortunate that it is being preserved as an historic site.

In the early 19th century, the frequency of shipwrecks along this coast increased as marine traffic burgeoned. After several bad wrecks at and near Cape Race in the early 1850s, a light was built in 1856 where the modern lighthouse now stands. It was made of cast iron with stone foundations and protecting walls, and it had a fixed white light. Its location on a headland put the light 55 metres (180 feet) above the sea, making it visible for about 32 kilometres (17 nautical miles) in clear weather.

The new light on Cape Race was a wonderful aid to seafarers, but shipwrecks continued, if somewhat less frequently. In December 1856, within the first year of operation, the *Welsford* hit the rocks below the light and went down with most of her crew. In April 1863, in dense fog, the *Anglo Saxon* broke her back on the jagged rocks just north along the coast and sank with the loss of 237 passengers and crew. In October of the same year, the *Africa*, another passenger liner, became a victim on the same rugged shore. When the *Assyria* crashed into nearby rocks in June 1901, most of the passengers and crew managed to get ashore. Her massive anchor turned up years later, and it now rests on the grass outside the keeper's residence. A recent map of known shipwrecks lists 360 names along the coastline around Cape Race.

Following the trend in other parts of the world, a rotating mechanism was installed in 1866 to give the light a characteristic flashing pattern. A deep-throated steam whistle boomed over the sea starting in 1872. One writer characterized a later diaphone-type horn on Cape Race as an awful noise.

Nowadays, electronic sounds have replaced the great bull horns of earlier times. Some of the early machinery and outside horns are preserved in the service building near the light tower. Rusting boilers and cinder heaps below the light also remind visitors of the light's long history.

The original tower and light lasted until 1907. By then it was clear that a new and more powerful signal was needed, so the old tower was dismantled and taken to Cape North on the tip of Cape Breton Island. The magnificent reinforced concrete tower that remains on Cape Race today was then built. It is some 6 metres (20 feet) in diameter and nearly 30 metres (99 feet) high overall, with a spiral stairway attached to the inside walls. A cast-iron collar about 2 metres (6.5 feet) high supports a lantern room 4 metres (13 feet) high with a riveted copper dome surmounted by a round ball and weather vane.

Cape Race's famous lightstation was celebrated in a commemorative stamp in 1937.

What makes it unique, however, is its four-faced Chance Brothers hyperradial lens system—the largest of its kind in the world and the finest available at the time. Each lens is nearly 4 metres (13 feet) high.

Nearly half a ton of mercury was used at Cape Race to float the 7 tons of glass and metal frames in the lens system. The entire apparatus revolves once every 30 seconds. In 1998, the old clockwork mechanism for turning the light and the massive weights to run the clockwork were still in place, but the light is now turned by a quietly humming electric motor.

Ships on the way to and from Europe passed not far off Cape Race on the great circle route, and they would sometimes pick up or drop off passengers and mail. At Cape Race, Newfoundlanders went out in small boats to catch the fast mail ships offshore. In 1858, the Associated Press of New York stationed a boat nearby to collect the latest European news that was dropped in canisters from the ships. Cape Race had connections to the telegraph network, and the news so gleaned reached New York and Boston long before the ships.

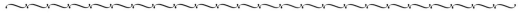

One of Cape Race's giant lenses.

Cape Race is also remembered for the Marconi station here that heard the distress signals from the crippled *Titanic*. The *Titanic's* remains lie some 3,600 metres (11,800 feet) below the ocean surface not far to the southeast.

In 1957, when the *Stockholm* rammed and sank the *Andrea Doria* off Martha's Vineyard, Cyril Myrick, at the radio on Cape Race, relayed messages from rescue ships. He is of the Myricks who have staffed the lightstation since 1874, a noteworthy family dynasty.

This great landfall light, with its massive tower and superb lens system, is a magnificent sight in fine weather on its bare headland with the sea all round. Notoriously dense fogs that cover the sea and land for about half of the year frequently reduce visibility to a few metres. With the spring or autumnal gales bringing driving rain or snow on winds well over 160 kilometres (100 miles) per hour, it is little wonder that this lighthouse is so sturdy.

The Cape Race lighthouse was declared a National Historic Site in 1974. This wonderful lighthouse is readily accessible from St. John's by following Route 10 south from St. John's, and turning east on a gravel road at Portugal Cove South, past impressive coastal scenery to the cape at the end of the road.

CAPE PINE

By 1850, lighthouses on the south coast of Newfoundland had become essential. After all, this area was on the north side of the main entrance to the Gulf of St. Lawrence, and, as geologist J.B. Jukes noted in 1841, the south coast of Newfoundland was "strewed with . . . properties and bodies" (*Jukes, 1842, Vol. 2, p. 187*). After debating responsibility with Newfoundland and Canada, Her Majesty's Government in London finally agreed to build a lighthouse at Cape Pine on the south end of the Avalon Peninsula, close to the southernmost point of Newfoundland. The name *Cape Pine* now seems inappropriate in view of today's barren landscape.

As was common during that century, cast-iron plates that could be bolted together were carried across the Atlantic in a sailing ship to a landing place below the site, lugged up the cliffs, and assembled. The structure stands to this day. The light went into service on January 1, 1851, with 16 Argand burners and reflectors rotating to produce a flashing beacon. The light was converted to acetylene gas in 1928, and in 1982 it joined the local hydro system.

Now it is an automated station with a simple rotating searchlight in the original tower and a spacious lamphouse with the keepers' houses nearby. Its daymark of three horizontal red bands makes an impressive sight from land approaches as well as from sea. Its automatic electronic foghorn calls across the foggy waters from a position well below the tower.

The Cape Pine lighthouse has been designated an historic site, but it still awaits restoration and maintenance. It may be staffed again sometime in 2003.

Cape Pine is readily accessible by road, about four hours' drive south from St. John's. Take Route 10 to west of Trepassey and then a marked gravel access road to the lighthouse, using the power lines as a guide. Resident sheep, wandering caribou, and occasional tourists are the only visitors.

CAPE ST. MARY'S

In 1860, Cape St. Mary's became the site of the third of a series of lighthouses on Newfoundland's south coast. From its lofty position 100 metres (328 feet) above the sea, the original brick structure supported a rotating light of a dozen burners and reflectors that, on a clear night, could be seen for 40 kilometres (25 miles). The present structure is a plain white octagonal concrete tower topped by a boxy-looking aluminum lamphouse with an automated rotating searchlight.

Cape St. Mary's, now an ecological reserve, provides one of the world's most spectacular bird-watching sites. From their cliffside nests, clouds of noisy gannets, kittiwakes, puffins, turres (or murres), terns, and gulls fly over the sea to their feeding grounds.

Cape St. Mary's is accessible from the coastal road, Route 100, around the southwest lobe of the Avalon Peninsula. A well-marked branch road leads to the bird-watching site and lightstation.

West Coast from Rose Blanche

Rose Blanche Point

In 1873, an unusual stone lighthouse and residence, all in one block, were built at Rose Blanche Point near the southwest corner of Newfoundland. This community, about 40 kilometres (25 miles) east of Port aux Basques, takes its name from *roche blanche*, French for the local "white rock." An engraving from that time shows a two-storey square house built of large rectangular blocks of stone with deep-set windows in its thick walls and a light tower as an upward extension of one of the corners (top right). Its beam, about 30 metres (98 feet) above sea level, was visible at sea for 19–22 kilometres (10–12 nautical miles), more than adequate for local fishermen and coastal shipping.

In 1873, John Roberts, an Englishman, became the first keeper. The lamps he maintained are reputed to have come from Scotland as lighthouses there were being modernized. After Roberts' tenure, five other families tended the light until it was decommissioned in the 1940s. Descendants of those families still live in Rose Blanche and nearby communities.

Closed up and abandoned after decommissioning, the old stone edifice fell into ruin. Since 1996, the Southwest Coast Development Association has painstakingly restored this old building and tower. Fallen stones in the ruins were catalogued and cleaned. Old photographs were enlarged and individual blocks recognized and numbered. About 70 percent of the original stone blocks were recovered and used in the restoration. To provide additional stones, a quarry was opened up near the original one just below the lighthouse. Meanwhile, a nearby square white skeleton tower, with a rotating bare light that turns itself on and off, provided a beacon for those at sea. A ceremony in August 2002 marked the relighting of the Rose Blanche Point light, the culmination of many years of work by dedicated volunteers.

Lighthouse lovers and those interested in Newfoundland cultural history applaud the restoration of the lightstation to its original condition. The site is accessed by taking Route 470 east to Rose Blanche from Port aux Basques and the ferry terminal.

Original lighthouse from 1873 publication.

Restored lighthouse, 2003.

CHANNEL HEAD

A lightstation was placed at Channel Head on an island on the west side of the entrance to Port aux Basques Harbour on the southwest corner of the Island of Newfoundland. When the Newfoundland Railway was completed across the island from St. John's in 1894, Port aux Basques became its southwestern terminus and the principal entry and exit point for travel between Newfoundland and Canada. Now, with the Newfoundland Railway but a memory, large modern ferries, each carrying as many as 350 vehicles, provide year-round service between Newfoundland and mainland Canada.

Each year thousands of people see the Channel Head light's slender white tower from the ferries at the entry to Port aux Basques Harbour. It was meant to complement another station at Cape Ray, 20 kilometres (12 miles) around the corner, built by the Canadian government in 1871. These lights were to bracket the entry to the Strait of Canso, along with those on St. Paul's Island off the north tip of Cape Breton Island.

The original lighthouse, of circular iron construction, was replaced in 1980. The current tower is about 8 metres (26 feet) high with a red band daymark, radio masts, and service buildings. Its booming diaphone foghorn, installed early in the century, was replaced with an electronic horn in 1980.

This station is not readily accessible, but it is visible from the ferry at Port aux Basques.

CAPE RAY

Concern about lighting the entrance to the Gulf of St. Lawrence around the southwest corner of Newfoundland resulted in the construction of the Cape Ray lighthouse in 1871. In 1885, the tapering tower, some 15 metres (49 feet) high, was destroyed by a fire that started in the oil lamps. It was immediately replaced and crowned with a typical Chance Brothers lamphouse and lens system (right). In 1955, another fire weakened the structure, and it was replaced with a concrete tower (above). Now it stands automated and alone with a searchlight on a topless tower and with most of the service houses removed. The location, however, is most unusual.

Geologists note that several principal faults separating portions of Newfoundland converge near Cape Ray. In addition, the area near the lighthouse has been the focus of archaeological attention in recent years after the discovery of several campsites dating from as much as 2,500 years ago.

In 1885, Cape Ray became the terminus of the telegraph line across Newfoundland and the connecting cable across Cabot Strait. In 1904, it was one of the first lightstations to be equipped with radio. Now fibre-optic cable, the latest in communications technology, passes through here.

To reach Cape Ray, take the Trans-Canada Highway north from Port aux Basques about 15 kilometres (9 miles) to the side road, Route 408, leading to Cheeseman Provincial Park and Cape Ray village. From the beach just beyond, a coastal road leads to the light. The Cape Ray lighthouse has recently been turned over to the Southwest Coast Development Association, the same group that restored the Rose Blanche Point lighthouse.

The Cape Ray tower, with its original lamphouse, damaged by fire in 1955.

Cape Anguille

Another of the lighthouses protecting the southwest corner of Newfoundland and the Gulf of St. Lawrence was built in 1908 at Cape Anguille, 30 kilometres (19 miles) north of Cape Ray. It was a buttressed concrete tower capped with a Chance Brothers lamphouse and lens system (below). Several service buildings included a large two-storey keeper's residence. In 1980, it was replaced by the present octagonal structure with a plain red lamphouse (above). The Cape Anguille lighthouse has recently been turned over to the Southwest Coast Development Association, the same group that restored the Rose Blanche Point lighthouse.

Take Route 406 from the Trans-Canada Highway near Doyles and follow it beyond the village of Codroy. The lightstation is to the left down a short side road and is visible before you reach the village of Cape Anguille.

Cape Anguille, 1955.

TROUT RIVER

Visitors to Gros Morne National Park on the western side of Newfoundland may leave the main coastal road, Route 430, at Wiltondale and take Route 431 to the southern part of the park. The road leads to Trout River in the midst of spectacular scenery. At Trout River, the harbour is flanked by flat-topped terraces showing former levels of the ancient sea.

A small lighthouse about 4 metres (13 feet) tall, located on the south point, is unique in that it sits on what was the ancient sea bottom when the glaciers retreated and ocean levels were higher.

7/04   NO LONGER LH — now range light

WOODY POINT

A small plain white lighthouse about 5 metres (16 feet) high stands at Woody Point. It overlooks what was the old ferry route for all northbound traffic to Norris Point and for traffic up and down the west side of the Great Northern Peninsula before the highway was built around the north side of Bonne Bay.

To find the lighthouse, leave route 430, the main west coast road, at Wiltondale. Turn east on Route 431 to Woody Point. At the junction where the road swings sharply left up the hill toward Trout River, the lighthouse is visible on the point straight ahead.

LOBSTER COVE HEAD ▶ ▼

Drivers along Route 430, Newfoundland's west coast highway, can see an easily accessible lighthouse station just north of Rocky Harbour. This is the Lobster Cove Head light, which was established to assist ships in the Gulf and on the north side of the entry into Bonne Bay. A neat round tower of small diameter and about 8 metres (25 feet) high is topped by a lanternhouse with an umbrella-like roof on the cupola and a large weather vane. Support buildings are on several levels of the rocky point with the tower connected to the residence by the typical Newfoundland covered walkway. It was built in 1897 and modernized in 1970.

The Lobster Cove Head lighthouse is readily accessible from a short side road off Route 430.

POINTE RICHE ▶

Just beyond Hawke's Bay, well north of Gros Morne National Park, a paved side road leads to Port aux Choix. From there, a gravel road leads to a major lighthouse built in 1871 on an accessible shore area at Pointe Riche.

Pointe Riche is an excellent example of a tapering octagonal concrete lighthouse tower and platform with a Chance Brothers multisided lamphouse and three layers of square glass windows. The lower lamphouse is circled by a narrow platform with railings. The tower stands with two very small service buildings on the bare point facing directly into the Gulf of St. Lawrence.

Lots of parking and easy access to the limestone shore make this an attractive place to visit. On the road in, an interpretive centre explains the history of the area, including an account of archaeological sites that date back thousands of years.

New Ferolle

A superb lighthouse stands on the northwest end of the New Ferolle Peninsula, off the main west coast highway, Route 430, halfway between Port aux Choix and St. Barbe. It was built in 1913 according to Col. W.D. Anderson's famous buttressed design. A white hexagonal concrete tower with ribs on the corners and a flaring platform is capped with a traditional round red lamphouse. The main platform with railing is supplemented for cleaning purposes by a narrow iron platform just below the multifaceted window level. An access ladder leads from the main platform to the domed roof with its ball and weather vane.

In the summer of 2000, the beautiful original Fresnel lens was still in place—a rarity in the automated lighthouses of Canada today. The view from lighthouse is straight out into the Gulf of St. Lawrence.

Amour Point (Pointe Amour)

The tallest lighthouse in Newfoundland was built in 1855 at Amour Point on the coast of Labrador, near the Québec border. This part of the route from the Atlantic into the Gulf of St. Lawrence has long been a navigator's nightmare, and shipwrecks have been common.

Even after the Amour Point lighthouse was built, wrecks were frequent along the foggy coast. The site is unique in that it marks the graves of two British naval vessels. HMS *Lily* foundered in fog in 1889 and HMS *Raleigh* sank after grounding in fog, taking 10 men down with her, in 1922. Bits of her rusting steel are still evident along the shore.

The lighthouse's round tower was originally faced with stone and then brick and cement. Finally, it was shingled. At the base, the walls are 2 metres (6.5 feet) thick and taper slightly with eight landings up to the light platform. The deep-set windows at each landing mark the walls in sets of four on opposite sides.

The white tower has one broad black horizontal band about two-thirds of the way up. The round lamphouse, with its characteristic railed deck and red cupola, housed a second-order Fresnel lens system, which has now been replaced by an airport-style rotating electric beacon. The double two-storey keeper's house is joined to the light by a covered passage.

This fine lighthouse is accessible by first taking the Route 430 up the west coast of Newfoundland to the ferry at St. Barbe. From there, cross to Blanc Sablon, Québec, an interesting voyage of an hour and a half. Local roads east along the coast bring you to the Amour Point lighthouse in less than an hour. The area is notable for icebergs in spring and early summer, all manner of seabirds and whales in season, and a procession of passing marine traffic.

Flower's Cove

Newfoundland's main west coast road, Route 430, passes on the landward side of Flower's Cove, north of St. Barbe, the Newfoundland terminus for the ferry across the Strait of Belle Isle to Québec and Labrador. The view from the highway over Flower's Cove village includes a lighthouse on Rocky Island to the north. It was constructed in 1899 with a catoptric light apparatus, and its light was visible for about 20 kilometres (12 miles).

The short square tower with its plain glass lamphouse is on the corner of a small square residence building with a chimney as tall as the light. It sits just offshore and can be viewed from side roads in Flower's Cove.

The Flower's Cove lighthouse operated until January 1969 and changed hands several times. It has been taken over by the Straits Development Association, now preserving it as part of a regional development scheme. Preservation involved boarding up the windows and doors, which were painted a bright blue, unique in Atlantic lighthouses.

Lighthouses

They stand exposed on lonely rocks
With crying gulls and breaking seas
On wooded points with patches of green
Small worlds from shore to trees.

Concrete towers, red caps aloft
That face the winds and furious seas.
Pyramids of wood with hidden strengths
In hand-hewn timbers and tamarack knees.

Lonely now with keepers long gone
Who climbed the stairs in dark of night
Uncertain that sailors were out at sea
Yet tending their weights that turned the light.

Empty houses and weed-choked paths
That led to light and horn
Rotting stairs and leaning rails
Once guides in fog and storm.

Watchers used to look for ships
From tower tops beside the light
As convoys of waves from distant storms
Broke on rocks in frenzied white.

Fishers still pass in tiny boats
While great ships far out at sea
Slowly cross the rim of the world
Lights to bring them home safely.

And always the sea, the source of life,
Friend at times but often foe
Sparkling blue in summer's sun
Sullen grey in driving snow.

Old lights stand proud, faithful still
With no one there, controlled afar,
Noble symbols of another time
Telling strangers where they are.

References and Selected Readings

Adams, W.H.D. *Lighthouse and Lightships.* London: T. Nelson and Son, 1871.

Bush, E.F. "The Canadian Lighthouse." *Canadian Historic Sites: Occasional Papers on Archaeology and History,* No. 9. (1975): 5–110.

Canadian Coast Guard, Marine Navigation Services. *List of Lights, Buoys, and Fog Signals.* Ottawa: Fisheries and Oceans Canada.
  –*Atlantic Coast,* editions 1987 and 1998
  –*Newfoundland,* editions 1981 and 1998

Cowper, William (1731–1800) *The Solitude of Alexander Selkirk*

Jukes, J.B. *Excursions in and About Newfoundland During the Years 1839 and 1840.* Vol 2. London: John Murray, 1842.

LaFrenière, N. *Lightkeeping on the St. Lawrence.* Toronto: Dundurn, 1996.

Molloy, D.J. *The First Landfall: Historic Lighthouses of Newfoundland and Labrador.* St. John's: Breakwater, 1994.

Palgrave, Francis T., editor. *The Golden Treasury of the Best Songs and Lyrical Poems in the English Language.* London: MacMillian, 1875.

Richardson, E.M. *We Keep a Light.* Toronto: Ryerson Press, 1945.

Richardson, E.M. *Our Other Islands.* Toronto: Dundurn, 1996.

Smallwood, Joseph R. *Encyclopedia of Newfoundland.* St John's: Newfoundland Book Publishers, 1982–1994.

Stephens, D.E. and S. Randles. *Discover Nova Scotia Lighthouses.* Halifax: Nimbus, 1998.

Stephens, D.E. and S. Randles. *PEI Book.* Nimbus Publishing, Halifax, 1998.

Talbot, F.A. *Lightships and Lighthouses.* London: William Heinemann, 1913.

Thurston, H. and W. Barrett. *Against Darkness and Storm: Lighthouses of the Northeast.* Halifax: Nimbus, 1993.

Whitney, D. *The Lighthouse.* Toronto: McClelland and Stewart, 1975.

Zinck, J. *Shipwrecks of Nova Scotia.* Vol 2. Hantsport: Lancelot Press, 1977.

About the Author

DAVID BAIRD was born in Fredericton, New Brunswick, and spent his early childhood abroad with his missionary parents. Returning to Canada, he settled in Saint John and later attended the University of New Brunswick. He received his Masters degree in science from the University of Rochester and his doctorate from McGill University. After a career teaching in eastern Canadian Universities, David Baird became the founding director of the National Museum of Science and Technology in Ottawa, and held similar posts at the Royal Tyrrell Museum of Palaeontology in Drumheller, Alberta, as well as the Rideau Canal Museum in Ottawa. In 1985 he received an Honourary Doctor of Laws from the University of Calgary and in 1986, he was made an Officer of the Order of Canada. Across the course of more than 40 years, he has visited and documented many hundreds of Canadian lighthouses.

Index of Lights